DISCIPLINE
IN THE CLASSROOM

Revised Edition

National Education Association
Washington, D.C.

> **Note**
> Previously published material used in this book may use the pronoun "he" to denote an abstract individual, e.g., "the student." We have not attempted to alter this material, although we currently use "she/he" in such instances.
>
> NEA Publishing

Copyright © 1969, 1974

National Education Association of the United States

NEA Stock No. 381-11878 (paper)
            12112 (cloth)
ISBN 0-8106-1325-5-00 (paper)
       0-8106-1330-1-00 (cloth)

Library of Congress Cataloging in Publication Data
Main entry under title:

Discipline in the classroom.

   1. Classroom management—Addresses, essays, lectures. I. National Education Association of the United States.
LB3011.D5   1974   371.5   74-13022

Contents

Introduction 7

Discipline: An Overview
"Discipline Is...." by Sister Helena Brand, SNJM. 11
"What the Books Don't Tell You" by Jane Tylor Field. 16
"A Positive Approach to Elementary School Discipline"
 by Frances Holliday. 18
"Classroom Control in the High School" by Emelie Ruth Dodge .. 21
"Secondary School Discipline" by Knute Larson — with
 comments by Frances D. Bartlett and Matilda Luney 25

Curriculum as Discipline
"Better Curriculum — Better Discipline" by William Van Til 35
"Operating a Free but Disciplined Classroom" by Daisy Bortz
 as told to Anne Hoppock 37
"Reading: Failure and Delinquency" by William C. Kvaraceus ... 41

Classroom Techniques for Discipline
"Matching Teacher, Student, and Method" by Louis J. Rubin. 47
"Cheating" by John Carter Weldon 53
"The Teacher and Preventive Discipline"
 by Adah Peckenpaugh. 56
"A Lesson in Discipline" by Teresa Foley 58

Methods of Structuring Classroom Behavior
"Behavior Modification" by the Staff of the Center for
 Studies of Child and Family Mental Health,
 National Institute of Mental Health 67
"A Positive Approach to Disruptive Behavior"
 by Teressa Marjorie Pratt 70
"The Disturbed Child in the Classroom" by Katharine F. Tift 74

Discipline and Human Needs
"Discipline Is Caring" by Alvin W. Howard 81
"My First Year of Teaching" by Wylie Crawford 85
"Embarrassment and Ridicule" by Lawrence E. Vredevoe. 89
"Wanted" by Henrietta M. Krahulik 91

Acknowledgments 96

Introduction

Old fashioned remedies and new-fangled therapy, common horse sense and sophisticated research—the articles here reflect a broad spectrum in their approach to discipline and the teaching process. Even though *discipline* is now called *classroom control,* these articles indicate that some educators question the desirability of precise prescription in the classroom.

Running through the articles is a common thread: discipline is less of a problem when the instructional content and process are interesting and relevant, constitute stimulating activities, and arouse natural curiosity. This use of broad and general terms in dealing with discipline problems could indicate a limited base of research or a lack of success in motivating students. Since, as many of the articles point out, what constitutes meaningful curriculum or stimulating activities for one student may be irrelevant for another, the matter of motivating individual students appears to be the critical problem. This is particularly apparent in those articles under the heading Curriculum as Discipline. William Van Til makes the point well when he says, "Better discipline will prevail when learning is related to the social realities which surround the child."

For Van Til, boredom and discipline problems are closely associated; he, therefore, proposes that "improving the learning environment of millions of Jimmy's . . . [will avoid] needless disciplinary struggles." However, in acknowledging that some students become disciplinary problems despite meaningful curriculum, Van Til opens the way for consideration of the various approaches recommended in the other articles. These range from an attempt to match a teacher's teaching style to a student's learning style, to a strict behavior modification where the forms of behavior—and not the attitudes behind behavior—are the primary concern.

One thing is clear from reading these articles—there are no final and pat solutions to the problems of discipline. Perhaps we shouldn't look for precise answers. But we should encourage ourselves and others to try out the alternatives presented here. Hopefully, the teachers who read this book will find some ideas they'd like to put into practice, some clues for innovation. And, hopefully, this book will give the general public a better background for understanding this important issue today, discipline in the classroom.

                        Bernard H. McKenna
                        NEA Instruction and Professional Development

Discipline:
An Overview

Discipline is . . .

Sister Helena Brand, SNJM

FORMULAS for maintaining classroom discipline are many and varied, and what works for one teacher fails for another. Chances are, nonetheless, that any formula that proves effective contains the following ingredients:

Discipline is preparation — long-range and short-range. Long-range preparation is the necessary, daily routine of planning, preparing material, and correcting papers.

Short-range preparation is the activity just before a class begins that results in students' entering an orderly room. The teacher has all the necessary materials ready for distribution. He has written key words on the board to guide students in following his instructions and to make oral spelling unnecessary. He adjusts windows, arranges his books, checks his seat plan, and prepares his attendance slip. The classroom is ready, and the teacher is in control. Class begins promptly without that little lull in which attention is often lost before it is even captured.

Discipline is dignity. In the classroom, the teacher lives his dignity by avoiding casual sitting positions, casual vocabulary, casual joking, familiar give-and-take — except when they are deliberately used as tools of emphasis.

Dignity expects the courtesy of a greeting when pupils come into the classroom. The teacher will not receive acknowledgement from every student, but his attitude will encourage many greetings.

Since the teacher expects the class to consider education a serious business, he approaches his class in a businesslike, professional way. He is courteous, considerate, pleasant, understanding, consistent, and, in the sum, dignified.

Discipline is moving deliberately and purposefully with the apparent self-confidence of a captain on top-deck. The disciplined teacher shows that he knows exactly what he wants to do. By acting serene, he creates an atmosphere of serenity. Students assume the matter-of-fact, reasonable, practical tones and attitudes of their teachers. Generally, a student is as tense or relaxed as his teacher.

Discipline in the Classroom

Discipline is speaking distinctly with a pleasant, friendly voice. Students will listen more attentively and ask questions more spontaneously if the "sound effects" are pleasant and harmonious. Tape recording a few periods and playing them back can reveal to the teacher poor speech habits, such as lack of tone variation or overly numerous "uh's," that detract from presentations.

The teacher who does not speak simply or slowly enough for his students to understand easily may find that students release their feeling of frustration and inadequacy by finding compensating entertainment. When a student stops doing what the teacher wants him to do, he begins to do what he is tempted to do.

Discipline is teaching a subject in terms of the interest level of the class. The vocabulary challenges at times, but it is within the understanding of the class. Good current allusions, based on newspaper or magazine articles, are attention-getters which act as springboards to new lessons.

Discipline is questions and answers from the students. A discussion sparked by a student's questions is usually lively because interest is tapped and channeled. The best answer is the student answer. The teacher whose students not only raise questions but reason their way to the right answers practices a special kind of personal discipline. He controls his very human tendency to save time by "just telling" the class the answers. The right answer formulated by the students does more for their development than the most dynamically articulated answer the teacher could produce.

Discipline is utilizing the natural tendencies of the students. Carefully planned group discussions and buzz sessions, or occasions when students plan and take responsibility for their own activity, give the students the chance to express their desires and clarify their purposes. They also allow the young people to experience the success of influencing their group and to grow in personal security. Such sessions give students a legitimate reason for speaking as opposed to reciting during a class period, and for moving to another part of the room.

Discipline is perceiving and understanding causes of misbehavior. The perceptive teacher notices the student who comes to class burning with resentment and rebellion. Aware that he may have had trouble at home that morning or in his previous class, the teacher avoids any conflict which will aggravate the student's sense of injury and result in sullenness, insolence, or even violence.

Discipline Is....

The teacher realizes that many, if not all, of his students suffer from feelings of inferiority or inadequacy. Particularly affected are those who may feel out of the "in-group" because they are of a different race or religion, because they lack money, or because they cannot keep up mentally or physically.

The wise teacher knows that publicly demeaning a student or in any way implying rejection or ridicule is inviting misbehavior, which is often a defense mechanism.

Discipline is realizing that students are human beings. Students leave books and pencils at home. (Teachers forget things too.) To punish a student's forgetfulness by keeping him idle is retaliatory rather than remedial. The youngster feels conspicuous, frustrated; above all, he feels a sense of injury. The better course is for the teacher to provide the missing article and thus have a busy rather than a humiliated student. The "little talk" for chronic amnesia victims can come at the end of the period when he returns the article the teacher has loaned him.

Being human, students appreciate recognition. They are happy to be in charge of something. They are proud to be sent on errands, glad to be noticed in the hall.

When papers are returned, a comment by the teacher praising a mark, remarking on the completeness of a particular answer, or noting the neat attractive format or script, not only excites ambition but also promotes a pleasant teacher-pupil relationship. The morning after a play, a recital, or a game, the student who is complimented on his outstanding participation is an appreciative, cooperative person.

Discipline is knowing when to tighten, when to loosen, and when to hold firm. A class changes its mood with the weather, with the exciting rally students screamed through during the noon hour, with the warm library period they have just sat out, with the way things went in the last class, with the pictures that appeared in the morning's issue of the school paper. Students come into the classroom with an attitude toward the teacher engendered, perhaps, by their success or nonsuccess with the assignment.

Sometimes students come in quietly, sometimes in a stampede, sometimes laughing, sometimes bitterly arguing. The bell momentarily cuts off their stream of interest, and into this small space the teacher drives the line of action he expects the class to follow through the period. He directs their vitality. By clear, simply spoken instructions he puts them to work.

Discipline in the Classroom

If directions offer personal advantages to the students as individuals, the class as a whole will settle down. An effective means to calm a class is to have written recitation during the first 10 or 15 minutes. The teacher remarks that the lesson is of more than usual importance. He wants to credit every individual who has done the assignment with a successful recitation. Since it takes too long for each student to recite, each may earn a recitation credit by choosing two of the four questions to write on. Even if they do not finish writing in the allotted time, the work they have completed will indicate the quality of their preparation and the papers will be scored with that in mind.

Another time, he may have the student decide on the question or topic he found most interesting and then write on it for ten minutes. Students set to work with an optimistic spirit, glad to put their best answers forward. Just before they begin writing, the teacher directs their attention to the next day's assignment on the chalkboard. He suggests that if they finish the class exercise before the time is up, they look over the new material. He will answer any questions on the new assignment after the writing session is terminated. He indicates that the rest of the class period will be a build-up for the assigned work. Looking to their personal advantage, the students generally cooperate.

Sometimes a class needs waking up instead of calming down. On Monday, perhaps, when students are recuperating from a busy weekend (or giving the impression that they had the kind of weekend that requires recuperation), a buzz session can be profitable. It gives students an opportunity to compare notes, improve their homework papers, argue, and wake up.

Discipline is anticipating difficulties. The misbehaving individual makes a problem for the teacher and also for the class. During the first month of school the teacher checks without exception infringements of class or school regulations. One individual who "gets away with it" breeds others who will try. Planning for emergencies and anticipating problems develops and maintains teacher control, strengthens students' confidence in the teacher's authority, and establishes a receptive classroom atmosphere.

Finally, discipline is having effective attitudes. Effective attitudes stimulate pupils to action. Creative thinking develops in the classroom of a teacher who shows that he appreciates a student's point of view. An instructor who is really thrilled with his subject effectively presents it as an intellectual adventure, a colorful dis-

Discipline Is. . . .

covery that induces similar excitement in his students. An instructor who shows interest in student affairs, who not only listens to student problems but contributes to their solutions, is an effective teacher in the classroom, in the conference room, in the give-and-take of a lunchroom situation.

Teachers' discipline is essentially self-discipline. The young teacher who is hopeful yet fearful, ambitious yet humble, idealistic yet practical, with everything to give, with everything to lose, will find his success in proportion to his ability to know himself and to use that knowledge in personal and professional growth.

What the Books Don't Tell You

Jane Tylor Field

WHEN THERE IS a deviation from standard classroom behavior — when something wildly funny or wildly infuriating or wildly frightening or just hopelessly pathetic happens, something that the education courses neglected to dwell on — what will you do?

The proper and specific action depends, of course, upon what the incident is; upon the person or persons involved, including you; upon your school administration; and upon your community. But there are certain things it should be helpful to remember.

First, do not let anyone know that you are shook up, either by hysterics, pity, or horror. In the classroom, you are mother, father, counselor, tea and sympathy all in one. You are expected to be a rock, no matter what. So, though you may be blancmange inside, make like obsidian for your audience.

Second, try to remember any relevant administration policy which may have been discussed in faculty meetings. If the incident is one of a type for which a formula has been worked out, conform! Do not try to set a precedent with new strategy: for instance, if smoking by students on school property is grounds for suspension, report any offenders immediately. This is no time to lecture on the possibility of cancer.

Third, if necessary, *ask* for assistance. The nurse, administrators, counselors, and the vast majority of your colleagues are willing to back you up or lend their special skills wherever needed, and teamwork has long been noted for its superiority over lone wolf efforts.

Along the same line, do not forget to call a parent-teacher conference if it seems wise to do so. After all, parents are people too. Sometimes they are impossible, but for the most part they are like their kids — willing to learn if they think they are hearing the truth.

They may have no idea that their offspring is the class clown or the class black sheep or the class sad sack. Certainly they will seldom be complacent about such revelations. Most parents are only too anxious to help their children be happy and successful, and they know that there is no truer maxim in the world than that suc-

What the Books Don't Tell

cess breeds success. Clowning, goofing off, pining away, and like activities use energy which should be put to more constructive use, and parents know it well.

Fourth, do not let a molehill into a mountain grow. Keep things quiet. Don't let everybody get into the act. Don't even let it become an act.

Fifth, be objective. Do not take personally anything that may happen, even if it is of an insulting or belittling nature. Remember that no matter how charming or marvelous a person you are, as a teacher you represent authority, and there are times when authority is resented for its own sake.

Sixth, if the event has been one where you were fortunate enough to make some child's life a little happier or more comfortable, do not dwell on that either. Which is to say, don't talk about it. Be discreet. Don't tell everything you know. Just remember the channels by which such results were accomplished in case you might want to go through them again sometime.

Finally, remember that there will be friction and irritation and pathos and laughter in any job that deals with people, and teaching is certainly one which does. Therefore new human problems will ever arise and old ones will be repeated. Regard them with humor if possible, profit by past experience, refrain from wasting physical or nervous energy on them, and conserve most of your strength for your biggest job, that of helping students to learn.

A Positive Approach to Elementary School Discipline

Frances Holliday

ONE OF THE MOST challenging and often one of the most baffling problems parents and teachers have to face is that of channeling the ceaseless activities of children into an organized pattern of self-controlled behavior.

When is discipline good? Is it a question of domination by a teacher, of obedience to orders, of complete self-direction? All of these philosophies have been followed, but is any one of them enough to accomplish our purpose? How do we know when we have attained the ultimate in behavior?

Domination probably plays a part in growth: If self-control breaks down, the responsible adult must be ready to control the situation. Certainly obedience is a part: a child who cannot obey cannot learn to control himself. Also self-direction, with the aid of expert guidance, is essential to growth.

No one approach can stand alone, however, for as we analyze the goal toward which we are striving, we are convinced that the only good discipline is that which is evidenced by a growing self-control. Good teaching, well planned by the teacher and leading to cooperative teacher-pupil planning, is essential.

No "class" in self-control can accomplish the task. On the other hand, when children live together and take part in carefully chosen experiences in which they have a voice, they may be on the way to standards of behavior which are acceptable in a democratic society.

But a philosophy alone is not enough. Teachers need to incorporate this philosophy into the lives of children. Many opportunities for doing this arise in the normal activities of the classroom. Here are a few concepts and suggestions which may be helpful in making good use of these opportunities.

- Cooperative making of rules as the need arises may gain the interest of children while teacher-imposed rules may create resistance.

A Positive Approach

- Discussion of behavior problems as they appear will probably develop attitudes and a social consciousness that may guide the children in future decisions.
- A day filled with stimulating activities will allow little opportunity for idleness and mischief.
- Helping each child both to lead and to follow a leader may help him attain higher standards of group behavior.
- Having a clear understanding of the acceptable limits of behavior can give children a feeling of security and hence lead to better behavior.
- "Please do this" tends to foster cooperation. Always make a positive approach.
- Well-established routine minimizes behavior problems.
- Creative participation in classroom activities strengthens a feeling of worth and reflects itself in self-control.
- Group and individual tasks that give the child added responsibility for his own actions aid in development of independence in attaining good behavior.
- Varying activities will give a wholesome change of pace. Interest is sustained when we alternate tasks that require high concentration with those that permit greater freedom of movement.
- Every child needs a feeling of success in some activity.
- Expecting one type of behavior today and another tomorrow leads only to confusion and discouragement. Be consistent.
- Health and comfort should be furthered in the physical aspects of the environment. When a child is comfortable, it is easier for him to be well-behaved.
- Plan for a quieting five minutes at the start of the day, after recess, and after lunch periods.
- Work at being the kind of teacher that children like and trust. Strive for firmness with fairness, sincerity with tact, sympathy without sentimentality, humor without sarcasm. Remember the importance of a pleasant voice and good enunciation.
- Keep in mind that misbehavior is valuable energy directed into the wrong channels. The remedy for misbehavior lies in redirection rather than in suppression.
- Separate children who seem to have a bad effect on each other.
- Do not humiliate a child or make him the center of attention by public reprimand. A private conference is more effective and allows the child to save face.

Discipline in the Classroom

- When a child's misbehavior disrupts the group, isolate him by having him sit apart from his classmates until he has a chance to cool off.
- Handle the normal range of misbehavior yourself, but don't hesitate to seek help for occasional problems that call for the skill of a pyschologist or other specialist.

These are only a few of the manifold opportunities that present themselves to the alert teacher.

As we analyze desirable behavior in a democratic society, we realize that the essential ingredient is consideration of the rights and feelings of others. Evaluation of growth day after day and taking a step at a time in the difficult task of attaining self-control should help children to attain that final goal — living harmoniously and purposefully together.

Classroom Control in the High School

Emelie Ruth Dodge

AS I STOOD BEFORE my first eleventh-grade English class many Septembers ago, a full-fledged teacher at last, I enthusiastically looked over the 30 pupils whose lives I was going to mold, and my heart sang, "Mine! These are mine! I can do anything I want with them!"

This power-mad era in my life was brief, but it was years before I realized that behind the silence and order of my first day of school were concealed 30 scouts reconnoitering enemy territory. In my case, the report must have gone back, "Sitting duck!"

I was unprepared to cope with problems in classroom behavior. I knew the history of educational philosophy; I was familiar with educational terminology; I accepted the principle of permissive atmosphere. But no textbook or lecture had dealt with flying missiles, strange noises from unknown quarters, out-of-control discussions, chronic tardiness, impertinence, effrontery, or any of the other devices for retarding classroom progress.

"Discipline," in its connotations of demand and punishment, of autocratic authority, went out of style about 25 years ago. But because to teach remains the paramount purpose of teachers, and since this purpose cannot be accomplished without classroom order, "discipline" is still necessary although it wears a new and prettier dress. We see it walking abroad as "control."

Superintendents demand teachers who can control students; boards of education dismiss teachers who lack classroom control.

What, then, can new teachers do to deal with problems of classroom control? Teachers colleges and textbooks have some helpful general discussion of the matter, although they seldom go into detail about methods. Articles in education journals may be useful, and advice from experienced teachers can provide aid.

However, since the very same classroom problem rarely arises twice, a pat answer or case history isn't of much value. Furthermore, each teacher's personality has a different impact on students, and, therefore, each teacher is forced to discover his own particular way of handling a problem.

Discipline in the Classroom

I have found that the most sensible way to handle the matter of classroom control is by not allowing problems to develop.

My brief but potent experience has revealed some general procedures which boys and girls have seemed to find fair and logical and which I find helpful in preventing unpleasant classroom situations.

Several recent surveys of what students consider as the characteristics of a good teacher list fairness as a first requisite. This sounds simple. However, fairness involves constant vigilance on the teacher's part, careful attention to consistency, faithful warning in advance, and several weeks of patient waiting while the students test and observe.

To say that a teacher is fair neither convinces students nor makes it true. Having dealt with adults for years, students have learned that adults are inconsistent, inattentive, moody, and capricious.

Adults have severely punished youngsters on one day for an offense which, on another, merely receives a reprimand. And knowing that every grownup has a weak spot, youngsters have coaxed their elders into or out of decisions, have gotten away with deeds under the noses of preoccupied parents and teachers, have successfully and fraudulently appealed to the sympathy of adults to win their desires.

In short, boys and girls are what they are because of what adults, advertently and inadvertently, have taught them in and out of the classrooms.

If you want to build a reputation for fairness among your students, these principles may prove valuable to you:

Don't threaten unless you can, and intend to, fulfill the threat. Don't promise unless you can, and intend to, fulfill the promise. It will take only one unfulfilled threat or promise to assure your boys and girls that you are no exception to their rapidly crystallizing conviction that adults are three-quarters hot air.

Don't break a rule for anyone unless the entire class can see that it is an emergency. There are times when exceptions must be made; but when these cannot be postponed and handled in private conference, the class should be allowed to see that an exception is necessary.

Stick to school rules yourself. Frequently, it is not required that you observe them; however, do not break rules or equivocate before your students. If an assembly seems a waste of time, you can accomplish no good by going to sleep, "cutting," or being obviously

Classroom Control

bored. If there is a tardy bell, observe it yourself. Don't wander into your classroom late and expect your status to excuse you.

Always tell students the truth. It is better to say that you don't think they need to know than to risk being caught in even the most innocent and generous lie, and you will be amazed at how much the class can accept and understand.

Your students will hang around after school to talk things over and will seek your advice on the most personal matters once they decide that you are honest. But if you are to win their confidence, don't condemn too quickly their sweeping generalizations or their denunciation of the institutions most of us cherish. They must question everything. *Let them!* You and I have decided what we think about a good many things. They have that same right. But when they ask you what you think, tell them the truth.

Keep your classroom rules short and simple. Don't establish long lists of dos and don'ts, but make five or six basic and inclusive statements and then stick to them.

Always make your demands clear to everyone ahead of time. Don't give a pupil a chance to say: "But I was absent the day you gave us that!" Write your requirements and assignments on the board to be copied into notebooks, or give out mimeographed sheets. Then make absolutely certain that these instructions are understood.

The students' second requisite for a good teacher is knowledge of subject matter. If your boys and girls respect you as a person who knows what he's talking about, who is widely informed, and who works hard and consistently at his job, your problems in discipline will be fewer.

Come to class each day prepared to utilize every minute of the period. As I think over the unpleasant situations I've experienced in class, I find that they almost invariably occurred because the students were not really busy.

At least three different types of activity during one 50-minute period, such as a spelling quiz, a 15-minute discussion, and a short lecture, will provide variety and will keep students too well occupied to engage in class-disrupting entertainment. Always plan more than you can do in a period, so that if you see signs of boredom and restlessness, you can switch your activity and again avoid difficulty before it occurs.

In spite of all this golden advice, you will probably find some disciplinary situations arising in your classes. These are best handled unobtrusively on an individual basis.

Discipline in the Classroom

Don't *ask* a student if he will stop an annoyance. He will feel compelled to answer you, and the answer will probably be impudent. Simply *tell* him to stop whatever he is doing and then go on with what you were doing at once without waiting for a retort.

Any red-blooded student is aware that his friends are watching to see what will happen. If you give him the slightest opportunity to answer back, he will simply have to do so. Don't appeal to him by suggesting or implying that he is different from the others, that he has more ability than the others, or that he may expect sympathy because he has a problem at home. Young people want to be treated as individuals, but not singled out as different—even if they are.

I have found that normal teen-agers deeply resent special treatment. For the most part, they do not understand why or how they get into painful situations, but they feel that in treating them as psychological cases, teachers and deans are exhibiting a total lack of understanding and are making a crisis out of a crocus.

Many high school students will play on the sympathy of their teachers at every opportunity and later kill themselves laughing at the teachers' credulity. This arouses students' contempt, which writes finis to classroom control.

Your consistent refusal to accept late work or to make exceptions on the strength of tales of woe will be accepted with sheepish grins if you turn them away with, "Stop it! You're breaking my heart!" Parrying with a light and slightly flippant touch is often successful, as long as your foil is not dipped in the acid of sarcasm. Refusal to take a wheedling student seriously does not mean letting him—or the class—think you're ridiculing or belittling him.

You should try to be pleasant, you may be amusing, but always be firm. Any new group of students probably will not accept the fact, at first, that you mean what you say. They will continue to search for weaknesses. Expect, too, that you won't be able to be perfectly consistent all the time.

But if students know that you are trying to be fair, if they can respect your knowledge and industry, and if they feel that you sincerely like them, they will be less interested in humiliating or annoying you, in retarding class progress, or in seeking amusement of an unpleasant nature during class time. In fact, given the right classroom climate, self-discipline will flourish in a gratifying way.

Students will feel increasingly secure in your presence as they become more sure of their ground. When they know what to expect, they will feel happier and more comfortable, and so will you.

Secondary School Discipline

*Knute Larson—with comments in
italics by Francis D. Bartlett and
Matilda Luney*

YOUTH is a mirror which reflects all the blemishes of adult society. Schools today are being asked to deal with increasing numbers of badly maladjusted youngsters, and there is little question but that discipline is far more difficult to administer in our secondary schools than ever before. That the school year passes with a minimum of difficulty reflects, in large part, the skill and dedication of teachers, counselors, and administrators. School successes receive little publicity, however, and every medium of communication highlights our failures.

Mrs. Bartlett: *A maladjusted youngster is not necessarily a disciplinary problem. My experience has been that this kind of student more often presents a problem in teaching than in discipline.*

The Importance of Understanding Adolescents

A working knowledge of adolescent psychology is essential to successful secondary school teaching. Every adolescent is subjected to a maelstrom of confusing pressures. He is growing rapidly. Conflicting values and double standards may trouble him. He is more strongly influenced by his peers than by adults, and yet his home life is of tremendous importance in shaping his attitudes.

Mrs. Bartlett: *I am not convinced that an adolescent is more strongly influenced by his peers than by the adults in his life. Superficially, in manners and dress, he may seem to conform completely to his group. But any intimate conversation with him will easily show that his values and standards are directly influenced by his family and his teachers. We are, I think, unduly afraid of challenging the family to assume some responsibility for the behavior of its children.*

Effective teachers and administrators understand all this and plan every learning experience accordingly. Most administrators are aware, however, of certain staff weaknesses in the knowledge of adolescent psychology and especially in the application of this

Discipline in the Classroom

knowledge. Principals can help remedy such deficiencies by expanding in-service education opportunities and by having appropriate books and materials readily available. Bringing in specialists grounded in practice as well as in theory is also helpful.

Miss Luney: *Principals are the key people in solving the discipline problem. If they are given real power by the board of education, their attitude, support, and help can make the difference between an atmosphere of cheerful work or one of riotous ignorance in a school.*

Mrs. Bartlett: *Books and in-service education and specialists have their place, but teachers get the most help from staff discussion of individual students. It is a great deal more useful to talk about "Charles" than to talk generalities.*

Administrators should encourage teachers to visit superior schools and superior colleagues. Visiting days with pay are quite customary, but many teachers fail to take advantage of them—particularly the ones who could profit most. The principal, therefore, should personally recommend this type of visitation and suggest schools to be visited. A brief report to a faculty meeting might well be a sequel to such a visit, time permitting.

Miss Luney: *Visiting days are of little help with discipline. An expert teacher has few, if any, problems and the job looks deceptively easy. Even bad classes are good when visitors are present.*

Teachers who seem to have trouble in getting along with certain students should be invited to confer with counselors and administrators about the problems of these students. Such conferences often lead to amazing improvements simply by providing a clearinghouse for ideas and suggestions.

Mrs. Bartlett: *Conferring individually with problem students can often clear up difficulties not solved in any other way.*

Miss Luney: *Having an experienced teacher advise and help a new one is an excellent way to turn an earnest novice into a real professional.*

Spotlight on the Lesson

The effective teacher always knows where the class is going and sees to it that it gets there. The starting point for all preventive discipline is a good lesson, carefully planned and skillfully executed. This planning involves the curriculum of the entire school system, the year's work in the specific course, the unit, and the daily lesson plan.

Mrs. Bartlett: *Here is the key to solving the problem. When lessons are carefully planned and skillfully directed, disciplinary problems practically disappear. Unfortunately, many teachers do not have time to plan, to prepare, to confer with individual students.*

Students who fail to see the relevance of what they are supposed to learn are not ready to learn, and students who are not ready to learn are a likely source of trouble. The reason they are not ready may be that material is being presented in an illogical sequence, which is confusing to them. While such a situation cannot always be quickly remedied by the individual teacher, it can certainly be improved.

Mrs. Bartlett: *I hope Dr. Larson is not suggesting that all learning in the classroom must have some immediate practical application to the student's activities.*

Miss Luney: *The children of our disadvantaged groups are difficult to motivate. I believe that holding reluctant learners in school until they are sixteen or eighteen only increases discipline troubles and encourages borderline delinquents to emulate their sullen disorder.*

This is not the place for reflections on pedagogical techniques, but I urgently recommend a sharp upgrading of the quality and quantity of classroom supervision as a means of obtaining better teaching in our secondary schools. Far too many American secondary school teachers perpetuate procedural errors simply because they have no access to helpful supervision from department heads, chairmen, supervisors, or resource teachers.

Miss Luney: *A well-taught lesson usually avoids discipline problems, but a classroom teacher needs training and authority to deal with unusual emergencies.*

If there exists a single organizational key to better schools, it lies in more and better supervisors of classroom teachers. Too many teachers become supervisors by sheer virtue of seniority; too many supervisors spend so much time on statistical reports that they have little time to supervise. Generally, supervisors are inadequately paid for their extra duties.

Supervision and in-service education are particularly important to the increasing numbers of beginning teachers we must bring into our expanding school every year. Even when these young peo-

Discipline in the Classroom

ple have a solid foundation in their subject fields and in the theoretical aspects of pedagogy, they still need attention—particularly in applying some of the tricks of the trade.

Mrs. Bartlett: *It is not just the beginning teacher who needs the supervisor's counsel. Sometimes the older teachers, being less malleable, are the source of real trouble in stirring up disciplinary problems. The supervisor should be an experienced and outstanding teacher who commands the respect of his colleagues. He should be capable of conducting the kind of in-service training which fits the needs of the particular school.*

Miss Luney: *Beginning teachers need day-to-day help by experienced teachers and administrators. Our best and most dedicated young teachers may quit from discouragement while less desirable people who do not try to teach may remain.*

Now that the beginning teacher has actually come to the firing line, he needs to be reminded of many of the things experienced teachers usually take for granted—for example, emotional control and the importance of not regarding misbehavior as a personal affront; importance of voice control, good manners, and appearance; dangers of popularity seeking; and hazards involved in use of sarcasm. The first year of teaching involves so much learning that only the most gifted beginners can absorb it all without substantial assistance.

Mrs. Bartlett: *Perhaps the most important characteristic the new teacher must acquire is selflessness. The adjustment required in making the transition from being a student to being responsible for many students is a hard one.*

The Slow Learner

The slow learner is a frequent source of discipline trouble. Although his problems may stem from a variety of causes, he is almost invariably a poor reader. He finds it difficult to comprehend abstract material and to apply any given principle to a new situation. By the time he has reached the seventh grade, he has been subjected to years of frustration, both at home and at school. Often he stops trying and makes up his mind to drop out as soon as he is 16; even the best school has great trouble in persuading him to make further efforts.

Secondary School Discipline

Mrs. Bartlett: *Since reading retardation is usually the main source of difficulty for the slow learner, it would seem wise to build his program around his reading. He should probably be taught by one teacher who integrates all subject matter and approaches it through reading training.*

Miss Luney: *I believe teaching machines are ideal for slow learners. The youngsters enjoy the repetition and the machines are not worn down by it.*

Many of the needs of the slow learner are similar in kind if not in degree to those of his age mates. On the other hand, he has special needs of which the teacher should be aware.

Mrs. Bartlett: *Schools should provide teachers who are specially prepared to teach slow learners. Alarmingly often, however, slow learners are handed over to the newest teachers because they are the least able to object.*

Some of the special needs of slow learners are:

    1. Individual professional evaluation. Mass testing has a tendency to make the slow learner look worse than he really is. Teachers need to know exactly what they are dealing with.

    2. A meaningful and appropriate curriculum. Learnings should be practical but not merely utilitarian. Material should be selected from social studies, English, mathematics, and science as well as from the nonacademic areas.

    3. Appropriate remedial instruction. Help in reading is particularly important.

    4. Success at some academic tasks. The slow learner needs to experience success within the framework of his limitations.

    5. Firmness and consistency. The teacher must never surrender in the struggle to keep the slow learner working up to his capacity. Sometimes the slow learner must be driven hard, and he should never have cause to feel that the teacher has given up. For academic subjects, slow learners should be taught in small groups (under twenty) whenever possible. In nonacademic pursuits, they should be placed in regular groups.

Mrs. Bartlett: *The slow learner is not really ready for the degree of self-direction which high school requires.*

The slow learner responds favorably to appropriate audio-visual aids if he has been properly prepared for the experience and if the essential learning is hammered home after the presentation.

Discipline in the Classroom

"Kid stuff" that outrages his sense of maturity should be avoided. Distractions in the classroom should be carefully minimized. Informality, under close control, is essential. It is most important for these youngsters to enjoy their classes. Going along with a reasonable amount of fun is far easier than trying to stamp it out.

Mrs. Bartlett: *Complete agreement here.*

The teacher should never mix discipline with academic penalties; slow learners have enough trouble with marks without adding further misery. On the contrary, one should look for ways to reward extra effort with extra credit to open up avenues of hope.

Frequent changes of pace are necessary because slow learners have a short span of interest. Routine is important, however, for it gives them a feeling of security. Their teachers can profit from the experience of industry by breaking lessons down into small, repetitive steps and by employing easy exercises for reinforcement soon after the presentation.

Mrs. Bartlett: *Perhaps I am confused by the words "change of pace." It is true that slow learners have a short attention span and that they need to be fed in small mouthfuls with time for thorough chewing. However, they do not react well to rapid shifting from one aspect of a subject to another. A whole period spent on the slow mastery of one piece of work seems to provide them with the most real satisfaction. They need an immediate feeling of accomplishment.*

Gifted Students

Surprisingly, gifted students sometimes cause disciplinary problems of the first magnitude. Such students have a low tolerance for repetition, poor quality homework assignments based on "more of the same," and a general lack of challenge in the lesson.

They need a pace that is suited to their nimble minds; they need content that calls for creative thought rather than mere parroting of facts. They are impatient with classroom repetition of facts that have already been learned by reading. Teachers must be aware of individual differences and interests and do something about them in making work assignments. Teachers should be reasonable about the amount of outside work they require of these students. The magic lies in *quality* rather than mere quantity. If every teacher feels duty-bound to load rapid learners with ever-increasing amounts of work, the net result may be rebellion.

Mrs. Bartlett: *I have seen little manifestation of disciplinary problems among gifted students when they are grouped homogeneously. My own observations indicate that if problems arise it is because the students have been allowed to feel special instead of specially lucky. They must be held to the responsibilities of their unusual endowment, never permitted the kind of freedom which is purely physical rather than intellectual. And they must be taught by the teacher who is willing to admit that some of his students are more intelligent (and better informed in some respects) than he is.*

Miss Luney: *Gifted students need adequate libraries. They devour the usual instruction in minutes and are able to go on to more advanced studies by themselves. It is good for them. All their lives they will find challenge in reading.*

Punishment

At many points in years gone by, school discipline has bordered on barbarism. This accounts, in part, for some anachronistic laws restricting methods of punishment in schools today.

Corporal punishment is currently stirring up a lot of controversy, and sentiment appears to be growing for a return to its use in school as a partial answer to the problem of delinquency.

I seriously question that corporal punishment is effective in the secondary grades, but I do not feel it should be prohibited by law on any but the local level and then only by school board action. Such laws can be used for dubious purposes by certain scheming students, and they are, in a real sense, an insult to a noble profession. Their very existence implies a lack of confidence in our teachers.

Mrs. Bartlett: *I do not believe that corporal punishment has any place in the secondary school. The adolescent child, however recalcitrant, has his peculiar brand of dignity. If this is destroyed, there can be real trouble.*

Miss Luney: *Corporal punishment may be of questionable value in the secondary grades, but its possibility is a strong deterrent. Exclusion from school should also be a possibility. More children are injured physically and mentally by fellow students in disorderly schools than were ever hurt by teachers.*

Other forms of punishment in common use in secondary schools are: the reprimand, which should be private if possible; the enforced, after-school conference between teacher and student; deten-

Discipline in the Classroom

tion, which should be limited to minor offenses; enforced labor, which must be handled with care; fines, which should be limited to library delinquency or similar offenses; payment for destroyed public property; temporary isolation in the classroom; suspension from class; and expulsion from school, which is usually used as a last resort. Properly handled in a spirit of much light and little heat, these devices have proven effective.

Mrs. Bartlett: *Whatever form of punishment is applied, it should be consistent and supported by the administration. There are times when no one person can handle a disciplinary problem.*

I am pleased that nowhere is it suggested that extra assignments should be used as punishment.

Some Basic Principles

The importance of the individual teacher's understanding of certain principles underlying modern school discipline cannot be overstated. Let me conclude, therefore, by stating some of these principles:

• Discipline policies should be in harmony with the total goals of education. The disciplinary procedures of a school should never become ends in themselves or be confused with the procedures necessary in other types of institutions. The first criterion applied to any school disciplinary procedure should be, "Is this a sound *educational* practice?"

Miss Luney: *In the present crisis, the first criterion should be — Is it effective?*

• Disciplinary policies should be in harmony with research findings — notably in psychology and sociology.

• Disciplinary policies should be in harmony with the principles of a democratic society; that is, respect for the rights and dignity of the individual and equal justice and humanitarian treatment for all.

• Disciplinary policies should stress the *responsibilities* as well as the rights of the individual.

• Disciplinary policies should be positive and directed to the goal of self-discipline. The emphasis should be on the benefits of good self-discipline both to the group and to the individual.

• Disciplinary policies should be primarily preventive, secondarily corrective, and never retributive.

Mrs. Bartlett: *I particularly like the last three statements.*

Curriculum as Discipline

Better Curriculum — Better Discipline

William Van Til

AGAIN AND AGAIN, school discipline problems grow out of a curriculum which does not make sense to the learner. A class in which academic content bears no relationship to the needs or the world of the learner is a breeding place for rebellious disturbances.

The thing that is wrong and the source of trouble, we often hear, is that the content is "too hard" or, less frequently, "too easy." But "too hard" and "too easy" assume that the curriculum content and method are fundamentally right, and only the level on which the instruction is pitched is wrong.

All too often, this assumption is fallacious. When the curriculum itself is trivial, academic, unrelated to the learner's needs, irrelevant to the social realities which surround him, the question of level is of little importance. The real villain is often the curriculum itself, not the level.

The importance of a meaningful curriculum is documented as occasional educators sponsor formal or informal research on discipline. After a continuing informal study of discipline was made by his faculty, the principal of a junior high school in Morris Plains, New Jersey, reported, "The number of discipline referrals to the office ebbs and flows according to the kind of job an individual teacher does in planning, motivating, and presenting the period's work."

Recently 38 practices associated with effective discipline were tested through observation of Baltimore teachers. Conclusions were "The practice of using all available equipment and visual aids to embellish and enrich a lesson so as to interest and promote the learning growth of pupils is closely associated with effective discipline. . . . The practice of presenting the subject matter in a vital and enthusiastic manner, of making the subject matter appealing so that . . . [it] acts as a check or control to incipient misbehavior, is closely associated with effective discipline."

Better discipline will prevail when learning experiences relate closely to the present interests and needs of children who see the use of what they are learning. Better discipline will prevail when learning is related to the social realities which surround the child.

Discipline in the Classroom

Better discipline will prevail when we practice what we preach as to respect for personality. Better discipline will prevail as we develop active student participation, creative contributions, social travel, and all else that fosters significant experiences. Better discipline will grow out of a better curriculum in a better society.

You may know a little Jimmy who is a discipline problem despite an apparently meaningful curriculum. So do I. But in our concern for nonconforming little Jimmy, let us not neglect improving the environment of millions of Jimmy's through gearing our curriculum to the lives of the young and avoiding needless disciplinary struggles.

Operating a Free but Disciplined Classroom

Daisy Bortz as told to Anne Hoppock

DAISY BORTZ teaches a fourth grade. She has about 30 lively children representing a good cross section of the community.

Daisy's classroom is a place where children do things. They come together as a total group to plan, to think together, and to enjoy, but much of the time they work in small groups or alone.

How can Daisy be sure they are all working and learning? How can she keep all the threads in her fingers?

Out of her great wealth of experience, Daisy has developed hard-won convictions about how to operate a free but disciplined classroom.

The best kind of discipline, Daisy believes, is achieved when children are deeply absorbed in their work. In a sense, the task imposes the discipline. Children act up when they are bored; stay busy when they see sense in what they are doing. From the opening of school Daisy works to promote the idea that learning in her room is going to be exciting.

On the first day, she has many things around the room to tempt the children to explore and think. Next to the aquarium and terrarium the children find books on how to start such projects. A book on animals of the seashore is placed near a cluster of sea shells. Miniature animals and birds — a little squirrel and its babies, a tiny sea gull — invite handling. Hobby books of various kinds are grouped on a rack with books on how to do such things as science experiments without purchased equipment. Easels and a typewriter are available for use.

As children first begin to produce, Daisy is careful not to impose her standards, for she knows how easy it is to discourage the children before they really take hold. At the start, she shows interest and appreciation. Later, she will help them evaluate in order to improve.

Daisy recalls the hardest class she ever faced, a group of seventh graders who had been the despair of teachers for years. One of the toughest problems was Jim, a big boy who could read only at the

Discipline in the Classroom

second-grade level. In an effort to make school interesting, Daisy set the boys working on electricity and motors. Jim had the job of mixing paint for a big mural. He "invented" a paint-mixing machine by attaching a paddle to a small motor. Activities such as these changed Jim and his followers from troublemakers to good group members.

Daisy believes strongly in planning with children and having the plans always before the group. This planning tends to organize the day, to prevent wasted time, and to put responsibility on children to use the time well. "I tell the children," Daisy says, "not to think I'm here just to keep order and tell them what to do. We all plan what to do; each one knows what he will tackle first; each knows how much time he has to work. I don't believe that children can work intelligently and responsibly when only the teacher knows what is to be done, and why."

If clean-up chores are finished five minutes before the buses come, children and teacher check plans to see how they can use this last bit of time.

The never-a-wasted-moment idea is important in a well-disciplined classroom, Daisy believes. Trouble starts when children have to wait. In Daisy's classroom, there is no standing in line. Children don't sit down in the morning and wait for morning exercises to start. As soon as a child comes in, he begins work on an uncompleted job or starts a new one. Usually at the end of the day, the class summarizes where it is, and teacher and children put a skeleton plan on the chalkboard for the following day.

Daisy believes that one important way to assure order in a classroom is to arrange the room as a real workroom. Work centers stocked with necessary materials are placed strategically about the room. Such an arrangement prevents the children from clustering in too large groups, and the children know without instructions where to find materials and where to work. The arrangement of desks in blocks conserves space for these centers.

Daisy also has a chart with the various classroom duties numbered. Little cards, each containing a number, are kept face downward and each child chooses a card. If he feels he is not yet capable of handling the designated job, or if he has already done this chore for a period of two weeks, he chooses another card.

Daisy believes it is important to know and understand her pupils. She holds a child conference before any of her parent-teacher conferences. In preparation for this, Daisy has each child evaluate his own progress. Sometimes he writes her a confidential letter

Free but Disciplined

about things he thinks he does well, things which are difficult for him, personal problems he has.

He feels he can write freely because his letter will be destroyed after Daisy reads it. This letter forms a basis for Daisy's conference with him in which he helps decide what she will say to his parents and what he'll work hard on during the months ahead. The child talks over the conference with his parents, who are then ready to talk comfortably when they come for a conference with Daisy.

But Daisy doesn't limit her communication with children to planned conferences. They learn they can come to her any time they need her. Sometimes they interrupt something which seems important. "But," says Daisy, "even in the middle of a class you have to look at a child's face and see how great his need is before you tell him to wait for a better time."

Daisy knows that children frequently are unhappy, make others unhappy, and do not learn well because they believe no one respects them or cares about them. She is convinced that children must feel good about themselves in order to be good.

She cites several instances of children who might have become discipline problems if she had not helped them to achieve self-confidence and self-respect. For example, when Philip first came to Daisy's class, he had the reputation of being a bully. Daisy soon learned, however, that he was a sensitive child and his bullying behavior was only a cover-up. "As I got closer to him, he came to understand that he did not need to prove himself to me, and I helped him find legitimate ways to stand out in the group. He became one of our most helpful members."

Larry was another problem. Obviously an unhappy boy, he had been the butt of jokes because of his "out of this world" behavior. Often when the teacher or children spoke to him, he did not hear them although he was not deaf. In her first conference with Larry, Daisy said, "You know, you have one quality seldom found in boys —you can really concentrate on what you are thinking about."

"I can?" He seemed surprised at approval of any kind.

Daisy discovered that Larry was deeply interested in space exploration. She encouraged him to work on projects in this area and supplied him with materials. He began to report and demonstrate during science periods. His reading skill, which had been much below his interest level, improved rapidly as he worked on materials of interest to him and as he began to earn status in the room.

Theresa seemed to be rejected by the other children. She was dirty and ill-clad, neglected in body and spirit. Daisy began by sup-

Discipline in the Classroom

plying towels, soap, and comb and helped Theresa unobtrusively with her grooming. Then she brought Theresa a pretty dress (which her niece had outgrown), suggesting that she wear it the next day when the class was to go on a trip. Theresa gained self-confidence from her attractive appearance and began to take an interest in being well-groomed. She also became interested in dramatics and won praise from the others for her creativeness. By spring she was an accepted group member, learning and contributing.

"I feel pretty good," Daisy says, "if by the end of November we really understand one another." Usually, by this time, the children know what to expect of her. She knows more about them, when to be lenient with them, when to tighten up.

Daisy believes the teacher must always be in control of the situation and must therefore set limits. She wants children to have all the freedom and responsibility they can take, as fast as they can take it, but no more.

"They have to know what I, as the responsible adult, expect. They have to learn what we believe in this room and why. I involve them in making the rules we live by, but once the rules are made, they must learn to abide by them."

Sometimes Daisy gets cross and shows it, especially when the children do foolish or unkind things they have previously agreed not to do. "I'm living with them in the classroom and I want them to know I care a great deal about how we live."

When a work group gets a little noisy or disorganized, she goes to the center of the disturbance, finds what is wrong, and does a little redirecting. Frequently a child who is starting trouble responds to her arm around his shoulder or a little rub on the head.

"I often sit on the big piano bench to work, and I'll beckon a child who needs to think a little to come and sit beside me. I make note of recurring problems, try to find reasons, and work with the child privately."

Daisy doesn't send a child to the office but sometimes arranges to go with him to talk things over with the principal, who is good at working with confused or disturbed children.

Punishment? Daisy doesn't seem to use it much. "I like children," she says. Liking is the first step to understanding, and understanding is the most effective means of creating a favorable learning climate in the classroom.

Reading: Failure and Delinquency

William C. Kvaraceus

Children who fail to learn to read and to achieve academically experience school as a kind of public hell. Hell is what they have come to expect, for hell is all they have ever known in school.

To the failing child who must cope with a threatening classroom environment, delinquent behavior often serves as a defense or device to maintain a measure of emotional comfort. It is no surprise that many poor readers and nonachievers take the dropout route, but it is surprising to note how many are able to hold on, persevere, and graduate.

Recent data gathered by the American Institutes for Research reveal that 60 percent of male delinquents and 48 percent of female delinquents graduate from high school. When one considers the nonpromising academic profile of most norm violators, it is obvious that someone in school—teacher, counselor, administrator, remedial reading specialist, psychologist—must be playing an effective role in understanding and supporting these youngsters.

Generally, these delinquent youngsters develop an early interest in driving cars, having dates, staying out late, and leading their groups in social and physical activities, but they are singularly deficient in academic achievement and tend to develop negative attitudes toward school and those who supervise them. These traits are associated either as cause or as effect in the delinquency syndrome, depending on the case.

Frequently, forces that compel delinquency may also account for failure to learn. It is also true that failure and frustration in school can result in norm-violating aggressivity that may bring the youngster to the attention of official agencies—police departments and courts. Whatever the causal relationship, poor readers and nonachievers must learn to cope with what may be an almost Dantesque school situation, in which they are forced to endure one ego-destroying year after another.

We shall consider a number of ego defenses that threatened youngsters employ in an effort to hold their own and to survive in school and that frequently evolve as delinquent or adjustive behavior. But, first, what are some of the statistics on delinquency and reading problems?

The 1970 White House Conference on Children pointed up youngsters' inability to read as a major educational problem. Recent data on the extent of the reading problem in the United States indicate that—

• One in seven elementary schoolchildren is sufficiently below grade level in reading to require special attention to keep up with her/his classmates; in the case of large-city elementary schools, the ratio is one in four.

• One in four 11-year-olds reads at or below the level of an average nine-year-old.

Approximately three out of four schools reporting pupils with reading problems provide some special reading instruction to assist these students.

Jumping to delinquency data: Between 75 and 85 percent of the youngsters who appear in juvenile courts and who find themselves in institutions and shelters are unable to read books and other material appropriate to their age and grade in school. A three-year prediction study *(Anxious Youth: Dynamics of Delinquency,* 1966) found that a significant number of junior high school youngsters who fall into the lowest reading group tend to be norm violators. Reading ability or disability, whether it be cause or effect, must be taken into account as a potential factor closely associated with the expression of delinquent behavior in youngsters.

Attention to the poorest readers at any grade level may enable a school to focus on a group of vulnerable youngsters who are already (or who will soon be) showing adjustive mechanisms that may get them in difficulty with authorities.

Generally speaking, school data on delinquents indicate that they are educationally bankrupt. Constant failure breeds frustration, and frustration can lead to aggression against self, against other persons, or against property.

What ego defenses and coping mechanisms are available to frustrated learners in their attempts to maintain themselves in an unfriendly environment? We shall see how a good offense is very frequently the best defense for them.

Caught in a book-dependent system, youngsters who have difficulty reading can resort to the following devices: hostility, identification, displacement, projection, and denial. Or they can withdraw and run away. When they act out these defenses through illegal norm violations, authorities classify them as juvenile delinquents.

Reading: Failure and Delinquency

If they elect to take the hostility route, failing and frustrated students often make the teacher their special hate object. For example, in a study of delinquency that was carried out by 10 delinquents who interviewed 100 delinquents, the teacher rather than the policeman is given as the one "who hurt me the most" or "who I hate the most."

Many teachers learn to accept such hostility in an impersonal way and to respond to it with help rather than with rejection. Such response may confuse the pupil who is more accustomed to a return of like for like or "an eye for an eye and a tooth for a tooth." But teacher acceptance of the hostile student may lay the groundwork for a fruitful relationship. If the teacher is not accepting and understanding, it is doubtful that the teacher can help the youngster learn or improve in behavior.

Failing pupils may set up their defense via the identification process. With this technique, frustrated and defeated learners who feel woefully inadequate as they face daily learning tasks may find strength and courage to live through their unrewarding hell by identifying with an older delinquent or a delinquent gang. On the other hand, they may find support by making a positive identification with a teacher or an ex-delinquent "who has made good." (This may explain the success of tutoring programs that use older students who had difficulty in learning to read or whose background is similar to that of their pupils.)

Unsuccessful pupils sometimes use displacement in their attempt to maintain some degree of emotional comfort in a threatening and unrewarding classroom environment. These students are often able to live out the school year by shifting their hostility from teachers, principals, and other school personnel with whom they have had anxiety-producing contacts to individuals in home and community who are not responsible for their anxiety.

Students resorting to displacement may indulge in personal insult and property damage to local citizens whose homes border the schoolyard. These youngsters may steal a purse, mug an unsuspecting old man, deface a building, throw a stone through a plate-glass window, or write obscenities on the sidewalk. Cold comfort though it may be to injured and justifiably irate citizens, this displacement process may offer some needed emotional relief to the students who engage in it.

Still other failing and frustrated learners may work out their emotional needs via projection. Not only do delinquents hate strongly but they carry a long roster of enemies. Pupils who are losing out often attribute the strong feelings of hostility and aggressivity they hold for themselves to the innocent victims of their aggressions.

Discipline in the Classroom

They may perceive school personnel, police, an achieving pupil, even parents as the attacker and aggressor—the enemy. Usually, school personnel hold the highest rank in the unfriendly army. Hence, delinquents may see their ownselves as martyrs or even saviors working against the hostile and offensive power of the school establishment.

When interviewed about their school achievement and norm-violating behavior, many delinquents tend to deny their own lack of success, aggressivity, and attacking behavior. "Who? Me? Not *me!*" is a frequent denial of reality.

In an effort to control superego and to allay feelings of guilt, they submerge the harsh truth via exaggerated fantasies. They see themselves as innocent victims of a school conspiracy to keep them captive—an unrewarded slave faced with every kind of preposterous academic task.

In reviewing the plight of poor readers and nonachievers and their frantic attempts to maintain some emotional comfort in the threatening classroom environment via projection, displacement, identification, hostility, and fantasy, it becomes apparent that delinquency may enable some pupils to hold on and to graduate. However, if the understanding and the support of significant others in school (teacher, principal, counselor, remedial tutor) are missing, these mechanisms may only serve to compound the failing pupil's problem and to produce a standard school dropout.

Classroom Techniques for Discipline

Matching Teacher, Student, and Method

Louis J. Rubin

It is safe to conjecture that on countless occasions a student has been shifted from one teacher's classroom to another's because a "personality conflict" arose. Researchers have long been interested in these mismatches, which cause child and teacher alike untold aggravation.

In the present way of things, students and teachers are assigned to one another arbitrarily; with luck—or with sufficient mutual tolerance—both usually survive the encounter. But mere survival, after all, may not be enough, for when child and teacher do not like one another, the quality of learning obviously must diminish. Thus, even when the learner and tutor manage to repress the discomfort which one may trigger in the other, life in the classroom still remains far less gratifying than it could be.

Personality conflicts are probably inevitable. To begin with, all of us have our special likes and dislikes. There was a time when we assumed that—properly trained—any teacher could work effectively with any child. Greater maturity, wisdom, and sophistication, we reckoned, should enable the truly expert teacher to accommodate to the peculiarities and idiosyncracies of even the most demanding learner.

It is now plain, however, that people, alas, are not so made. Moreover, in recent decades, the relationship between teacher and student has become a good deal less formal and more permissive. As a result, even the protective insulation formerly provided by custom and clearly defined roles no longer exists. Today, not only does a child usually forego saying, "Yes, sir," or "No, ma'm," but is also likely to quibble about the usefulness of an assignment or the logic of the teacher's decisions.

And, beyond likes and dislikes, humans tend to have very different preferences with regard to the ways in which they go about their affairs. We speak, for example, of "night people" and "day people." Some individuals are heavily dependent on routine, some have a great dislike for the unexpected, and some prefer to go about chores randomly rather than systematically. Obviously, differences of this sort often complicate the relationship between student and teacher. When, by the luck of the draw, the behavioral styles of the student and teacher blend, the student can be herself/himself and thrive happily in the classroom. When, however, behavioral styles contrast sharply, one must either adjust to the other, enduring the consequent irritation, or the two must separate.

To compound matters further, all of us are subject to our special distortions, our private stereotypes, and our individual irrationalities. Whereas one teacher believes that children should be seen and not heard, another is disturbed by excessive docility. Some teachers are particularly annoyed by those personality characteristics in their students that they hate in themselves, while others are extraordinarily understanding and sympathetic with such students. Some teachers may be exceptionally sensitive to certain actions in children: cheating on a test, perhaps, or chewing gum or talking back.

For all of these reasons, then, the forced partnership between teacher and student sometimes takes a heavy toll in emotional agony.

An obvious question therefore arises: Is there some way in which teachers and children can be matched for compatibility? Can we find a formula for a successful school marriage between a teacher and a child, so that the relationship is mutually rewarding and relatively tension free?

The evidence from social science research, though not yet conclusive, almost certainly leaves room for modest optimism. The sheer mass of humanity in the school would alone almost guarantee that, given suitable matching devices, children could be placed with teachers of similar emotional makeup, thereby substantially reducing personality conflicts.

The critical problem, of course, lies in the discovery of the matching devices themselves. How, in short, can we predict which child will do best with which teacher?

Several years back, when I was director of the Center for Coordinated Education on the Santa Barbara campus of the University of California, we carried out a rather interesting experiment. Borrowing some ideas from Lee Cronbach and Abraham Maslow, we were impelled by the notion that "natural style" ought to be a significant factor in professional training—rather than fit the person to the job it might be more efficient to fit the job to the person.

We conjectured that we might be able to match a teacher's style with an instructional method that was particularly fitting and, going a step beyond, connect both of these with a student who also had a high affinity for the same teaching method. We knew, for example, that teachers can devise alternative instructional programs with which to accomplish the same objective, that most children learn more easily with one kind of method than with another, and that teachers usually prefer a particular approach in working with children. We assumed, in short, that theoretically it should be possible to join all three elements in such fashion that maximum congruence and compatibility would occur.

We assumed that if we could match teacher, student, and method, positive gains would result. Children would learn more effectively and find the process of learning more enjoyable; student-teacher personality conflicts would be reduced; and teachers would find their work more satisfying. Furthermore, we hoped that such matching would greatly reduce the range of problems with which teacher in-service education must cope.

Represented graphically, the conception we used would resemble the illustration below.

Teacher	Method	Student
Mr. Jones	A	Lisa
Ms. Smith	B	Beth
Ms. Douglas	C	Jenna
Mr. Carter	D	David

Assume, for example, that we have four different reading programs at our disposal. The illustration suggests that Mr. Jones has a strong stylistic preference for Method C, and a student, Beth, also seems to learn most effectively with Method C. Hence, by allowing Mr. Jones to use Method C and by assigning Beth to his class, the harmony among teacher, method, and student should improve.

Couched in the form of a question, the purpose of the experiment might be stated as follows: If a teacher has a natural teaching style, can it be conjoined both with a pupil's natural learning style and with a particular teaching method so as to achieve minimum incompatibility among the three?

One other facet of the experiment is also worth noting. We launched the investigation when the open classroom movement was ascending in popularity. We were convinced that should an open classroom have only a minimal degree of structure it would be unsuitable for some teachers and for some children. We were not opposed to the movement as such; indeed, we believed that under proper conditions, open classrooms had much to offer. We thought it likely, however, that some teachers, because of their particular personality bent, might not work effectively in the absence of routine and, similarly, some children, too, might be upset by a lack of classroom structure.

In retrospect, the study was a bit less than ideal, partly because of some technical limitations but chiefly because of the difficulty in finding distinctively different instructional curriculums aimed at precisely the same teaching objectives. All in all, however, we obtained results which we regarded as reasonably significant.

Our procedure was comparatively simple. We began by creating six short social studies units dealing with six social problems: segregation, race, hate and violence, poverty, cultural pluralism, and the future.

Next, we employed a group of 10 outstanding, experienced, and highly regarded teachers to create teaching guides for the six units. Each guide specified learning materials to be used, the reasoning skills to be learned, and the social values to be encouraged. In addition, it provided a precise teaching strategy as well as a set of learner activities that could be used with each of the objectives. Put simply, the classroom obligations of both teacher and student were well organized beforehand.

This done, we solicited the involvement of sixth-grade teachers. Members of our staff called upon interested teachers and demonstrated two versions of the experimental curriculum: one (involving the use of the guide) was highly structured and the other (offered to the teachers without the guide) was comparatively unstructured. Our staff advised the teachers that both models were useful, that neither offered a clear-cut advantage over the other, and that outstanding teachers used both approaches. After examining the models, the teachers selected one or the other on the basis of their stylistic preference. In effect, then, we gave the teachers an opportunity to use either a detailed course of study, carefully worked out in advance, or basic units which called for the spontaneous invention of teaching strategies.

In this way, we obtained 45 teachers who had a strong stylistic preference for preplanned teaching and 45 who preferred to develop their own teaching procedures as they went along. Each group agreed, for the purposes of the experiment, to use the selected methodology for the duration of the project.

Because very little research has been done on style in teaching, the need to compare the effects of one style against those of another posed some difficulty. We know, for example, that children learn in different ways and that teachers use different methods, but we do not yet understand fine details which separate one style from another.

After a review of various alternatives, we concluded that the phenomenon of anxiety lent itself to the kind of exploratory study we wished to make. Previous research had shown that highly structured learning programs frequently produce better performance in high-anxious children. Low-anxious children either do better in a comparatively unstructured program or perform no differently under the two conditions. We could find no research that compared the teaching styles of high-anxious and low-anxious teachers, but we conjectured that a similar relationship could exist: High-anxious teachers might prefer and accomplish more with a preorganized program.

It seemed feasible, therefore, to use anxiety level as a way of getting at individual variation in style. Since stylistic preferences in teaching probably are linked to personality variables, we could capitalize upon what was already known about the relationship between anxiety and the desire for situational control and examine stylistic inclinations among teachers.

We chose sixth-grade children in California primarily because they had recently taken intelligence tests and their scores were available. (Since intelligence and anxiety have a slightly negative correlation, it was essential to avoid a wide disparity in the pupils' intellectual capacity.)

At the outset, every student was given the Sarason Test Anxiety Questionnaire, an easily administered scale yielding a reliable indication of anxiety level. In a group of 30 or more youngsters, the odds are great that some children will manifest a high degree of anxiety, while others will be relatively free from undue tension. We assumed, therefore, that every teacher would teach both kinds of students. This proved to be true.

Children who say they are anxious about tests and other school activities may or may not be anxious in a particular class with a particular teacher. Hence, it seemed desirable to collect from the children periodic statements about their anxiety levels. An 11-item questionnaire (How I Feel About This Class) was created for this purpose. All teachers gave various forms of it to their students at intervals throughout the experiment. The evidence thus generated enabled us to judge whether the structured curriculum, because it was certain and systematic, reduced anxiety.

Another major aspect of the experiment concerned teacher staff development. As suggested earlier, we conjectured that if teachers could successfully be involved in instructional programs that were uniquely suited to their stylistic preferences, the problems of teacher in-service education might be greatly reduced. Hence, a considerable portion of the experimental activity involved a comparison of the results obtained when teachers are trained in an instructional program contradictory to their preferred style and when they are trained in an instructional program compatible with their natural style.

Our findings yielded a mixed bag. Although there were notable exceptions, spontaneous planning by teachers did not raise the stress level of anxiety-prone youngsters, largely because sensitive teachers tend, almost intuitively, to take compensating steps. We did determine, on the other hand, that the absence of reasonable structure imposes an emotional hardship on some teachers. But, surprisingly, these tensions do not seem to reduce the learning accomplishments of the teachers' students. One is forced to conclude, consequently, that good teachers care enough to overcome whatever handicaps they meet.

On the debit side of the ledger, however, a problem of some importance did emerge. We found that the classroom interests of children and their teachers conflict sharply. Children are interested less in knowledge than in emotional success: They want to be popular, liked by the teacher, regarded as good students, and adept at classroom activities. They learn — in many instances — not because they value the intellectual gain but because they seek the rewards which come from such gain. They want, in short, to be psychological winners.

Teachers, in contrast, are most often valued by their administrators according to the amount of information their students learn. Thus, they are of necessity more interested in the learner's cognitive success than in the learner's emotional success. Seemingly, then, there is a profound need to strike a better classroom balance between the mental and emotional aspects of schooling.

Finally, with respect to the matter of teaching style, we were, happily, close to the target. Teachers do vary in the ways they go about their tasks, and they do find some tactics considerably more comfortable and efficient than others. While their styles are not immutable, they have a deep-seated preference for curriculums that fit.

Every teacher, in a sense, has a particular cup of tea. Since children too seem to prefer one blend to another, we would be well-advised to search for arrangements that place both teacher and learner at the right table.

Cheating

John Carter Weldon

AN ALMOST unnoticeable but periodic tap, tap, tapping at the back of the room during a test gradually penetrated my professorial mind. Joe and Mac, who I knew had been in a communications unit during their military service, were using the International Code and their pencils to help each other with the questions.

It was my duty as a teacher to stop their ingenious cheating, but if I accused them directly, they could look innocent and pass it off as nervous pencil drumming. An old Navy signalman myself, I waited till Mac sent his next plea to Joe, then tapped out, "The answer to 27, Mac, is C."

Looking up, I met their startled glances squarely with a smile, and they grinned back, a little feebly.

Joe and Mac were grown men who must have been mature enough to realize, after my unspoken rebuke, that cheating hurts only the cheater, for they went on to become conscientious students.

It is not often so easy to "cure" cheating, yet it is a problem every teacher must face even though he knows that only a minority of his students are susceptible and that very few become inveterate cheaters. The discerning teacher understands that a basic cause of cheating is the student's lack of confidence in his ability to stand upon his own two feet.

Cheating is a delicate problem, best corrected by tact and diplomacy exercised in ways which do not harm the student or jeopardize his position as an accepted member of the class. If it is necessary to speak to a student, private counsel is always better than public reprimand.

Sometimes a negative nod of the head is sufficient to prevent a student from cheating. Moving him to another seat is a temporary yet helpful remedy. Intermittently rearranging the entire seating plan of the class helps, but it removes the honest student from a location in the classroom he has become accustomed to, and it may cause unwarranted distraction for him during tests because of his unfamiliar surroundings.

Before students succumb to the temptation of cheating, they should be counseled and convinced that a student who cheats hurts not only himself but everyone around him. They should be taught to respect their classmates and to honor their rights and privileges.

Methods used to correct cheating practices *after* they have begun are often severe and not too successful. Sometimes, depending on the individual student, the teacher may decide to nip cheating in the bud at its first evidence, and the student may learn more from this decisive action than he could from all the counseling the teacher can offer.

Generally, however, the direct action method tends to set up behavior patterns with contrary effects. The student, often responding through his defense mechanisms, misinterprets remedial tactics and welcomes the recognition he is getting from his teacher and the notoriety his fellow students inadvertently award him. Feeling, perhaps subconsciously, that he must live up to his reputation, he may tend to become a habitual cheater.

The wise teacher, I believe, is one who tries to avoid student cheating by building the right class and individual attitudes.

I used to think that counseling students about cheating at the beginning of each semester would be sufficient. That was a mistake. Twice a year is just not enough. Experience has proved, furthermore, that talking about cheating becomes pointless when it is nothing more than mere reiteration. It must capture the student's eternally wandering imagination; it must be varied with a positive degree of fascination.

Guidance in the classroom must contain ample manifestations of friendship and understanding, the student must feel that he is held in unqualified respect, and he must have an honest desire to understand and to cooperate with his classmates.

Here are some reminders I have heard employed when test papers are distributed on exam day:

"If you feel an urge to copy, make sure you get the right answer. Your neighbor can be wrong, you know. It's absurd to copy *mistakes!*"

"Only one copy of this test is needed from each student, so you do not have to accept the responsibility to turn in your neighbor's work. You turn in yours, and let your neighbor struggle along the best he knows how!"

And for the student who has a tendency to copy because he is "all tied up":

Cheating

"If you're knotted up inside or you can't think straight today, stand up, stretch your limbs as far as they'll go — without going into orbit, of course! It'll help you do your own work better."

Now although these reminders are somewhat facetious, they do not pointedly threaten a single student, cast undue suspicion upon anyone, harp upon the traditional "If you cheat, I'll skin you alive!" or "Cheating is wrong" theme. They serve to relieve the student of a natural disposition to be nervous before an examination, and they help lift all students above the cheating level.

The Teacher and Preventive Discipline

Adah Peckenpaugh

I'VE BEEN TOLD that more teachers leave the profession because they cannot—or fear they cannot—maintain discipline than for any other reason. This seems particularly unfortunate in view of the fact that few students, proportionately, cause disciplinary problems.

Before any teacher allows this small minority to send him into a tailspin, he should face three simple facts: Every teacher has to deal with difficult students; there are no set formulas for handling them; children are not born "bad," and "badness" doesn't just happen.

The best cue for action lies in the third point: Avoid the development of behavior problems by practicing preventive discipline. This requires a growing, or at least a constant, ability on the teacher's part to recognize promptly the signs that may portend trouble. Which students are characteristically inattentive? Consistently fail to cooperate? Are careless in dress and manners? Seem overly anxious to gain recognition? When such signs appear, investigate their causes and start corrective measures.

No one thing does so much to keep students on good behavior, especially in the higher grades, as does an atmosphere of work and study in the classroom. Every pupil knows he is there to learn. Don't let him forget it, or succeed in making you forget it. Don't be afraid that you will lose your popularity by firmness. Sticking by rules never costs the teacher an ounce of student esteem as long as the rules are fair and are adhered to consistently.

But a businesslike classroom need not be a humorless one. Keep your sense of humor at all times, and tell a funny story now and then. You don't have to preface each lesson with a joke, but use a good one occasionally to break the tension and show that you are human. And you can be human without being familiar or allowing students to become familiar with you.

There is a great difference, of course, between the familiar and the personal. It is important to be genuinely interested in each student.

The teacher, to be sure, cannot control the size of his classes, nor can the principal, in many cases. Yet the administration can help

Preventive Discipline

by keeping classroom interruptions to a minimum and by trying to avoid late-afternoon scheduling of difficult subjects.

Even in larger classes, however, the alert teacher can build bridges between himself and his students by treating each one as an individual and by responding to the requests each one makes.

Often children may be reached by your showing an interest in their hobbies. A project assignment can be related to a hobby, and an occasional inquiry about the youngster's guppies, for example, can help you establish rapport with him.

All right — I know as well as anybody that the quiet reminder that works wonders with sixth-grade Sally may roll right off Joe Blow's leather jacket as he swaggers through the high-school corridors. So, if Joe swaggers into real trouble, don't be afraid to discipline him, or to send him to your principal, or to call his parents into conference. But don't make Joe feel that parents, principal, and teacher are in league against him. Hear his side of the story. Encourage him to offer his solutions.

If his parents lack the ability to face their son's problems constructively and cooperatively, abandon this avenue of help — but don't abandon Joe. He will need you more than ever then. You may be the most helpful adult with whom he comes in daily contact.

We should remember that boys' and girls' behavior cannot be separated from the behavior of people in general. While we are trying to teach our students to think, we are also, consciously or unconsciously, setting them an example. But never put on an act for them. Be sincere, be consistent, be firm, and be friendly.

A Lesson in Discipline

Teresa Foley

WE WERE A TERRIBLE CLASS. Every class likes to remember that it was pure hellion, but the thirty of us who started under Miss Gallagher at the Down School near the Buick garage really were terrible. We came along just when the argument between the phonics people and the associationists was at its height. We went at reading for three years by the word-recognition method and then in the fourth grade the teacher insisted that we learn to read all over again by sounds. We were also caught in the controversy over manuscript and cursive writing. And we hit the crisis in arithmetic.

In the beginning of the fifth grade, we were forbidden to use brackets in finding the lowest common denominator. We had to go click-click to an equivalent fraction instead, seeing all the pieces of pie in our heads. This meant that nobody at home (Who had Gestaltists in their families?) could help us any more. But, willing sneaks, we drew brackets with furtive fingers on our pants legs.

Child-centered psychology burgeoned in our town at this time. We were allowed to do some ridiculous things in school because we wanted to. When our parents heard about them, they were furious at first. Then they decided that the school must know what it was doing, and they let us do the same things and worse at home. Finally, like beer chasers after an evening of Mickey Finns, came comic books and television.

Every year for six years we grew stupider and lazier and fresher and more obnoxious. No one ever separated any of us, or kept any of us back, or adulterated us with new blood. We were a terrible package, referred to by certain members of the PTA as "Les Misérables."

Then came the seventh year and Miss Barracombie.

She was new to the school that year, so we did not have the usual case studies on her from previous classes. Her looks might

A Lesson in Discipline

have given us a clue, but we had always known amateur, experimental teachers so we did not recognize the career teacher when we saw her. She was perhaps fifty, tall, square-shouldered, and erect; neither feminine nor mannish, merely healthy and strong. Her face was handsome but not pretty. She had no subtle expressions: she smiled outright, she frowned outright, or she concentrated. Her voice was not harsh but had a peculiar carrying quality, vibrating longer than most. Eugene Kent took off his hearing-aid after the first day.

She greeted us that day as no teacher ever had. No talk of adjustment here, no plea for growth, no challenge to find ourselves. She said:

"My name is Virginia Barracombie and it will be Miss Barracombie to you indefinitely. One of these days you will meet someone from the last school in which I taught. The worst that he tells you about me will be true. It's a far cry from child to man, and it's not through games that we get there. You and I are bound together in a contract for one year: I teach; you learn. Behave yourselves and pay attention and this will be one of the good years of your lives. You have a minute to prepare yourself with ruler, compass, pencil, and paper for a review of the meaning and use of decimals."

It was the shock treatment all right—but with economy, with the clarity of piano keys struck singly, above all with authority. We had neither the opportunity nor the mind to look across the aisles at each other until recess. We were at work in the first five minutes— we, who always had a period in which to get ready to get ready. It was a blow to our unit pride, but we were less cohesive after the long summer and temporarily distracted from getting together on what to do about it.

We thought at first that we were just going along with her in a momentary tolerance. She was novelty, and among teachers that was hard to find. Then we found ourselves bound in a work routine. At that point some of us tried to bolt.

In its reactions to Miss Barracombie the class divided into four groups. Several of the nicer girls and a couple of the boys who had strict scholastic accountability to professional parents went into her camp almost immediately when they saw that she was systematic, skillful, and just. Another group, whose names and faces are always hard to remember, went along with her because they sensed that she was a stronger personality; that balking would be tiring, involve exposure of weakness, and end in failure. These two groups accounted

Discipline in the Classroom

for perhaps two-thirds of the class. In the remaining third were the Idiot rebels and the Hard-nut rebels.

The Idiots moved in first, without seeing where they were going. For example:

Idiot: "Do we *have* to put our names on our compositions?" (looking around at the other Idiots for appreciative laughter).

Miss B.: "You don't *have* to."

Idiot: (Next day after papers had been passed back) "I didn't get my paper back. I haven't no grade."

Miss B.: "Did you expect one?"

Idiot: "You said we didn't *have* to put our names on them."

Miss B.: "That's right. You don't *have* to walk around with your eyes open, either."

The Idiot sat down, uneasily. That afternoon his name was up with the absentees who had to make up the composition.

The Idiots were beaten from the start. She was indifferent to petty annoyances, and they did not dare try big ones.

The Hard-nuts, the long-time heroes, waited more patiently, seeking their own ground. Their particular dragon in the case of Miss Barracombie was her good sense, which forced an antagonist to assume a role so foolish as to threaten his status among his classmates. This forced the Hard-nuts to try to operate outside the teaching periods, in the rather limited areas of truancy, ground rules, and personal relationships.

It was difficult to challenge her with truancy because there our parents were solidly on her side, and besides, the occasional absence or trumped-up tardiness of an individual did little to alter the steady civilizing routine. As for opportunities on the school grounds, Miss Barracombie supervised only in her turn, and was by some unexpected quirk more lenient than any of the other teachers, letting us proceed at games considerably rougher than we wished to be playing.

The worst of the Hard-nuts was Lennie Sopel. He was big and tough and bearded already, very much in the know about engines, baseball statistics, and older women. He had a way of muttering wisecracks half under his breath when girls recited. At first they reached only to people in the surrounding seats. Then one day as Lila Crocker went down the aisle, Lennie said in a loud whisper that shook the room like an east wind, "Oh, man. I wish I had that swing in my back yard!"

Miss Barracombie stopped listening to a girl at the study table. The girl stopped talking. Lila fled to the waste basket and back to her seat, her face scarlet.

A Lesson in Discipline

The room became as silent as a tomb in a pyramid.

Miss Barracombie looked at Lennie for a long time, and he locked eyes with her, ready for a showdown.

"What are you thinking about, Lennie?" she asked at last, rather softly for her.

"Nothin'." He could say that one word as though it were the nastiest in the language. "Absolutely nothin'."

"Well, I'm thinking about something," she said still calm and relaxed. "You come in at three and I'll tell you about it. In the meantime, stand up."

"What for? What'd I do?"

"Stand up, please."

Lennie hesitated. Again it was one of her simple inescapable requests. He slid out into the aisle and stood up.

Miss Barracombie went back to her work with the girl at the table. Lennie started to sit down once, but she gave him a steady eye and he straightened up again. He had to stand by his seat throughout the rest of the afternoon. We kept looking at him, waiting for him to say something; Lennie couldn't seem to think of anything to say.

She kept him after school forty-five minutes every day for six months. He never spoke out of turn again in class and he never missed a session with her. It seemed a heavy punishment for one remark, and we couldn't get over either her giving it or his taking it. When we asked him what he had to do, all he would say was, "Nothin'. She just gives me hell."

"For forty hours, Lennie?"

"Who's countin'? And whose business?"

Then one day Alice Rowe gave us the lowdown. She had been helping in the inner office when the intercom was open to Miss Barracombie's room.

"She's teaching him to read."

Nobody would believe her. Lennie's in seventh grade, everybody said. He knows how to read.

"No, he doesn't," Alice said. "I heard him stumbling over the littlest words up there. Who's ever heard him read in class?"

We tried to remember when we had heard Lennie read. He was a transfer to us in the fourth grade, and there hadn't been much oral reading since then.

"How does he do his other work?" we asked.

"Who says he does?"

61

Discipline in the Classroom

    No wonder Lennie couldn't fight her. She taught him in secret the one thing he needed to have to give up cheating and pretending.

    The truth was, no rebellion had a chance with her. She wasn't mean and she never struck anybody (although our parents queried us over and over again on this point, wanting, we thought, to be able to say, "Of course, she has order! She whips them.") No situation could come up that she would not know how to handle efficiently and without damage to her single drive: she would teach; we would learn.

    Whatever we studied, we mastered. Of course, she knew the ones of us who could not connect with the main lines she was trolling, but she put out other lines for them and they mastered, too. Nobody was free not to learn. We were free to fail, but somehow a failure was not a separate thing, only a step in learning. She never assumed that we had achieved. She probed and exposed until she read it in the blood. A week later when we were not expecting it, she would check again. She was the only teacher whose grades on our report cards we never questioned. Nor would we let our indignant parents go to her. She knew.

    This was no love affair between the class and Miss Barracombie, however. She was businesslike and not tender with us. She encouraged no intimacies and the thought of confiding in her as we had in Miss Tondreau who used to love us in the third grade was wholly ridiculous. We were just different with her. When our special teachers came and Miss Barracombie left the room, Eugene Kent would replace his hearing-aid, and we would be at once on the Plain of Esdraelon, stalking a world of enemies. By the end of the period our specials would be limp and distraught.

    We did no better left on our own. If Miss Barracombie stepped out of the room—something she wisely did rarely—we would hit the ceiling. After all, we had been indulged for years. Thirty near-simians don't slough that off in a few stretching months. We had never been convinced that discipline comes from within, and when the restraining presence was removed we reverted to the barbarians that we were.

    Miss Barracombie never mentioned our behavior with other teachers or when she was out of the room, although the specials must have complained bitterly. It seemed to be part of her code that she was responsible when she was with us and others were responsible when they took us. We liked that. Miss Barracombie did not lecture or make us feel guilty. There was nothing to lecture or feel guilty about. We behaved. We learned. We had to: it was the contract.

A Lesson in Discipline

But the final lesson we learned from Miss Barracombie was one she did not try to teach us. It was during the last period. We were in the midst of a discussion on the use of quotation marks. The intercom box pinged on the wall and the principal said:

"A telegram has just arrived for you, Miss Barracombie. Will you send a boy down for it?"

She sent Herbert Harvey Bell. He was in the corner seat by the door. He went out running because she knew exactly how long it took to get to the office and back and he did not want to answer for loitering.

He returned with the telegram, gave it to her, and took his seat.

She opened the envelope calmly and neatly so as not to tear the inside sheet. Still reading it, she turned about slowly so that her back was toward the class. Her hands lowered. We could see that she was no longer looking at the telegram but at the bulletin board. She did not turn back to us. She kept looking at something on the board.

Then before the alerted, somehow apprehensive eyes of the class, Miss Barracombie began to grow smaller. It was in her shoulders first. They began to narrow, to go forward. Her back curved. Her head dropped. We waited, not knowing what to do. Herbert Harvey Bell seemed to feel the most responsible. He looked around at all of us with a question in his wide, stunned eyes. We had nothing for him. Herbert Harvey pulled himself up from his seat and ran across the hall to the teacher there.

Lennie Sopel had started down from his seat, but when he saw the other teacher, Mrs. Hamilton, coming, he turned and went back up the aisle.

Mrs. Hamilton went up to Miss Barracombie and peered into her face. Then she bent to the telegram still in her hands.

"Oh, my dear," she said and put her arm around Miss Barracombie. Miss Barracombie did not move. Her shoulders were gone, melted into her narrow back.

Mrs. Hamilton turned her in the direction of the door. Our teacher put both hands across her face and, huddled and small, walked out like a child under Mrs. Hamilton's arm.

No one breathed or moved. A few minutes later Mrs. Hamilton looked into our room.

"Miss Barracombie has lost someone dear to her, boys and girls. Try to finish the period quietly."

No one came near us for the rest of the afternoon, not even to dismiss us. But we did not behave as we usually did when left alone.

Discipline in the Classroom

Most of us took out our composition notebooks and pens. Some just sat there.

We were frightened—a little sad for Miss Barracombie, of course—but mainly frightened, and frightened for ourselves. If she could be struck down, who was so tall, so erect, with all things under control, what could not happen to the rest of us who never had any control on the inside, who had to be made by others to hold our shoulders back?

We were the best we had ever been until the bell rang that day. For a moment we could see our connection with adults. Through a maze of equivalent fractions and common denominators we could see other people, huddled and shrinking, being led out of strange rooms. And their faces were ours.

Methods of Structuring Classroom Behavior

Behavior Modification

*Staff of the Center for Studies of Child and
Family Mental Health, National Institute of Mental Health*

In the winter 1972 issue of Mental Hygiene, Daniel G. Brown discusses behavior modification and behavior therapy. A consultant with the Phoenix (Arizona) Area Indian Health Service, Mental Health Branch, Dr. Brown says this new kind of therapy, called variously behavior therapy, operant-conditioning therapy, or reinforcement therapy, has many promising applications for the teacher in the classroom as well as for parents in the home.

Basically, behavior therapy involves strengthening desirable behavior and weakening or removing undesirable behavior in human beings by the systematic use of learning theory and principles of conditioning.

A major part of behavior modification involves changing conditions that have maintained a child's maladaptive behavior. The theory of reinforcement learning holds that both desirable and undesirable behavior are learned or unlearned by the same process.

Efforts to modify behavior follow two major paths: (a) developing, accelerating, or maintaining desirable behaviors, and (b) weakening, decelerating, or eliminating undesirable behaviors.

In his article, Dr. Brown points out that undesirable behaviors may be reduced or eliminated through the use of such consequences as: positive reinforcement (reward) for the nonoccurrence of the undesirable behavior; negative reinforcement (e.g., punishment or isolation) for the occurrence of the undesirable behavior; or no reinforcement of any kind for the occurrence of the undesirable behavior (e.g., complete ignoring of such behavior).

In contrast to the traditional view that maladaptive behaviors are "symptoms" and surface manifestations of underlying emotional disturbances, the behavior-modification approach assumes that such behaviors are simply learned ways of adjusting to the environment —that these behaviors are determined by the consequences that follow them. While the traditional mental health professional seeks to uncover and deal with the original causes of undesirable behaviors and the individual's emotional response to them, the behavior thera-

Discipline in the Classroom

pist concentrates on altering environmental conditions and the present consequences of such behaviors and "symptoms" themselves which constitute the so-called disorders.

What are the classroom applications of behavior modification? How can the teacher usefully and appropriately apply principles of this therapeutic, educational approach in the classroom?

The following eight basic principles of behavior modification can apply to the classroom situation:

• Behavior is learned when it is consistently reinforced.

The teacher can reinforce an adaptive behavior. For example, when the teacher consistently thanks a child for assisting in distributing reading books, the teacher reinforces the child's helping behavior.

The teacher can decelerate a maladaptive behavior. Whenever Tim, who is a first grader, bites or hits his classmates, his teacher calmly restricts him for a short time in the time-out alcove where he can receive no social reinforcements, such as attention or encouragement from the other children.

The teacher can ignore maladaptive behavior. When a child curses in class, the teacher ignores the remark and calls on or walks over to a pupil who is behaving in a socially acceptable manner. Later, the teacher gives the offending child social reinforcement when she/he is behaving in an acceptable manner.

• The specific behavior that requires acceleration or deceleration must be identified and the child's strengths emphasized.

If children do not seem to be functioning up to their individual potentials, the teacher can define a reasonable improvement plan for each one. For instance, slow readers can keep daily scores and earn a token reward for daily progress in reading speed and comprehension, which in turn can be redeemed for a larger reward later.

• Behavior-modification planning must initially anticipate small gains.

The teacher should reward each improvement the pupil makes at the beginning of the program until broader gains are within the child's grasp. For instance, the teacher can give a token reward to the pupil who has difficulty with long division as soon as the child succeeds, let us say, in dividing the first digit correctly. As the pupil learns the process, the teacher can award tokens only for completely correct quotients.

• The consequences of behavior must be meaningful to the student.

In the case of adolescents, the teacher may use such reinforcements as leisure time or social room privileges. For instance, a fail-

Behavior Modification

ing eleventh grader improved his attitude toward school when the teacher permitted him to go to the social room after he satisfactorily completed each assignment.

- Consequences, rewards, or punishments must follow the behavior immediately.

The child who clowns in the classroom is reinforced when the child's peers giggle at her or his antics. To combat this, the teacher can send the child to a quiet corner along with a work assignment as soon as this behavior begins. However, when the child is working productively, the teacher can reinforce quickly with a pat on the shoulder, a token, or verbal support.

Many teachers plan activities that permit a child with particular interests to win peer approval. When a teacher recognized that Susan seemed withdrawn for several weeks, he capitalized on her artistic ability and gave her major responsibility for an art show. At the culmination of the activity, Susan stood beaming in the center of the young artists.

- Reinforcements may be physical or social. The type varies with the child's age and needs, the situation, and the teacher's plan. Many teachers have found that rewarding a child with a token of varying value can change a habit. Others use praise.

- Purposes and goals should be clear.

If possible, student and teacher should agree together upon a target behavior and confer on progress toward the goal. When the teacher reproached Jim about pushing other children on the playground, the boy agreed to maintain a chart on his pushing behavior. At appointed times, he and his teacher met to check on the chart. The ultimate reward for Jim's overcoming this behavior was a field trip.

- In each instance, the target behavior should be the best one for the particular student. The aim of behavior control should be self-control.

Behavior modification used to manipulate student behavior has potential for benefiting the teacher rather than the student. (Does Ms. Jones modify Paul's noisy behavior to promote Paul's well-being or to relieve her daily headache? It is important that the teacher use behavior modification legitimately for changing Paul's behavior in order to help him resolve his own problems — while often benefiting the teacher as well.)

A Positive Approach to Disruptive Behavior

Teressa Marjorie Pratt

In an eight-week experimental classroom at the Malcolm Price Laboratory School, University of Northern Iowa, two of us boldly ventured forth to do some prescriptive teaching with 10 intermediate grade boys who had a history of disruptive behavior in the classroom.

From the moment the boys walked through the door, we used contingency management techniques. At first, in order to gain cooperation and to reward success, we offered candy and trinkets, but we tried to phase out these tangible things as quickly as possible and move to relying on praise, free time, and the intrinsic rewards most students feel when they complete a task and do a good job. This is the story of the experiment as seen from the eyes of the teacher.

We divided our room into a work area and a free-time area. In the task area, the boys were expected to be quiet and to work individually at their seats on a task that had been prepared and was waiting for them when they arrived. On their desks they had a work record card containing approximately 120 empty squares. They earned check marks on this card for working quietly, for raising their hands when they required help, for completing tasks, and for ignoring any disruptive behavior in the room.

After they had worked a certain number of minutes, a buzzer rang, and the boys who had earned two rows of check marks on their cards could go to the free-time area. We required those who hadn't to stay in the task area until they had. When a new work period started, we gave these boys a new task, and they had an equal chance with everyone else to earn the two rows of check marks needed for the next free-time period. Some boys who earned more than two rows of check marks in a work period continued to work, for a total card of check marks could be turned in at the end of the day for a tangible reward, such as balloons, marbles, or other similar items.

When the program began, we had available in the free-time area a record player and records, some tape recorders, a wooden trampoline, many games and puzzles, all kinds of art materials, filmstrips with viewers, and plenty of books. In this area, the boys were free to

Disruptive Behavior

choose their own activities; and unless a boy misbehaved, he remained in free time until the lights went out, which was the signal to return immediately to the task area, sit down, and begin work once again. We gave check marks to the boys who behaved appropriately in free time and extra check marks to the first four boys who walked quietly to their seats and started work on signal.

We made use of another area—a "time-out" room where we placed any student whose behavior was so disturbing to other members of the class that it could not be ignored or any student who refused to cooperate at all with a teacher request. A student stayed in the time-out room until we felt he could once again return to the classroom and do his work satisfactorily.

We completely individualized our academic program for each student, using structured materials that required little or no explanation. The boys used teacher-made work sheets, commercially made workbooks, programmed readers, and skill texts. Their assignments were commensurate with their ability, for we wanted them to meet success after success. Every morning we wrote the work schedule on the chalkboard so all the boys knew what would take place during each time slot. Then they all worked on the same type of activity at the same time but at their individual skill levels.

My assistant and I had many trying moments. The boys were difficult to manage, and we found that some of their objectionable behavior, such as talking to each other during work periods, tended to feed on itself. We tried whenever possible ignoring a misbehaver, while at the same time encouraging those students directly around him who were behaving appropriately. We also tried to announce just why we were giving one person check marks and not the other one. An example would be, "John, this is for working so quietly and ignoring Joe's remarks." Sometimes, though, we had to give direct orders or remove a boy from the area.

All our boys had average intelligence but had been unsuccessful in school because of inattention and inability to settle down to a task. Thus, one of our most difficult jobs was to gradually increase the difficulty of work and to make it rewarding for the students to stick with one task until completion. We always gave check marks for completed work done correctly, and the number of check marks varied depending on the difficulty of the task.

Much of our energy went into adjusting the social environment so everyone would be able to work. This involved ignoring certain behaviors, rewarding others, and sometimes having a direct confrontation. Decisions had to be made quickly and with a display of confidence, but they also had to be reasonable and enforceable or the program would certainly have broken down.

Discipline in the Classroom

An example of decision-making might involve a boy who refused to work.

One of the boys once declared: "I ain't goin' to work on that paper, Mrs. Pratt!"

"That's up to you, John," I said, "but it is the only paper you'll get check marks for at this particular time," and then I walked away. We found it best to assume a matter-of-fact attitude and to say as little as possible.

The boy then might do one of several things. He might start to get up and wander around the room slamming things or poking other people. He might try to get back to the free-time area. After sitting and pouting for a few minutes, he might begin to work. Or he might sit and pout for the whole period, in which case, when checkoff time came, he probably would not have earned enough check marks to go back to free time. Happily, I can report that as time went by the boys seemed to do less pouting because they realized that they needed check marks in order to earn free time.

What would we do if the boy took the first alternative I mentioned and got up from his seat and began poking people or slamming things? Order him to his seat, probably. If he didn't go, we would tell him a second time and then tell him to go to the time-out room. If he would not walk to time-out, we would put him there forcibly.

One of the hardest things to do was to learn to ignore the boys who were yelling at us or demanding our attention in an inappropriate manner, particularly if they had worked well for most of the period. For instance, one of the boys might raise his hand but at the same time call loudly, "Mrs. Pratt, Mrs. Pratt, come check me off." If I paid no attention and just went and helped somebody else, he might yell again, "Mrs. Pratt!" If I still paid no attention, he might turn around in his seat and mutter something about my being a "chicken butt." Eventually, though, he would usually raise his hand and wait for help without yelling.

Sometimes, getting the boys' cooperation required quick thinking. Our part-time helper reported such an instance. One day she was on the playground with the boys, and two of them didn't want to come in. She knew that if she started ordering them in, she might just have more trouble. So, with the stopwatch in hand, she simply said, "Let's see if we can make it an Indianapolis 500 to the door," and the boys took right off.

At the beginning of the program, one of the biggest problems was caused by the boys' trying to mind each other's business. One boy in particular made a real nuisance of himself until he found that his

Disruptive Behavior

interfering only caused the other boy to receive more check marks for ignoring the taunts and aggressive behavior.

We also had some problems in the free-time area with destructive behavior and with things disappearing. Even with two of us working in the room, a lot of things were broken or disappeared. We tried to watch fairly closely, and if a boy was destructive with equipment, we sent him back to the task area. However, we finally had to remove some equipment, such as tape recorders, microphones, and some of the filmstrip viewers, because they were being mishandled.

We were not always in disagreement or at odds with the boys. We had lots of fun with them, too. We often played checkers with them and talked to them during free time about their interests, and we heard some interesting stories about fishing trips, popular music, trips to other cities, sports, and science experiments.

All in all, we were greatly encouraged about how children can be moved toward specific goals and about how their behavior can be modified to enable them to take advantage of the instruction they receive. This teaching method helps teachers become more consistent in their teaching. And it makes them more aware of the good things that the pupils are doing because they take note of this in a measurable way by using check marks.

The students, in turn, find out just how much academic work and appropriate social behavior they are capable of and they realize that they, too, can be successful. After all, don't the check marks show that? Soon, they don't need the reinforcement of getting trinkets or candy that the teacher has bought. They can earn the free time to make something really worthwhile, and before long even the free time becomes secondary as they get that certain "glow" we all like to feel when we have completed a task and know we have done a good job!

The Disturbed Child in the Classroom

Katharine F. Tift

If you are assigned a student whose daily actions foul up the learning climate in your classroom, you must, at times, have feelings of frustration, and even of fury. The purpose of this article is, first, to reassure you that you are *not* inadequate because you wish the child would disappear forever and, second, to suggest specific ways for dealing with problems which arise because the child does not disappear.

One note of clarification: If the comments which follow seem overly simple, it is because emotional illness is overly complex. Little attempt will be made here to analyze the causes of emotional disorder; rather, the goal is to provide practical suggestions for dealing with those surface behaviors which disrupt your classroom.

Try to visualize a "typical" disturbed child. DC is a ten year old whose social behavior much of the time is at a three-year-old level. The minute your back is turned, DC runs her/his pencil across a neighbor's worksheet, dips water from the fishbowl into the clay barrel, or shoves and trips others without warning. This child keeps you on edge because of her/his destructive actions but masters just enough subject matter and conforms just enough to your demands to keep you from telling your principal: "Either DC goes or I do." (A transfer is impossible; the other teachers have DC's, too!)

When you first get such a student, a useful step is to check with other staff members who have already come in contact with DC. Does your school counselor have a case record for DC? Did *other* teachers find DC disruptive in *their* group situations?

If their answers are No, put aside this article and, instead, ask a peer whom you trust to visit your classroom for a day. Tell this person (a colleague?) to observe *your responses* to the youngster, rather than vice versa. If your friend's findings lead you to seek guidance for *yourself*, be thankful for the experience! As you acquire insights into your own feelings, everyone — especially you — will be the winner.

The Disturbed Child

Once you feel confident, however, that you are not largely responsible for this "enemy" action in your classroom, take the next step of acquainting yourself with the general nature of DC's disease. What *is* emotional disturbance? Where does it come from? In what different ways does it manifest itself? For meaningful answers to these questions, try the following activities:

1. Read at least one book which deals with the emotionally disturbed child in the classroom. Several good books have been written in this subject area; three, which many educators recommend, are the following:
    a) *Conflict in the Classroom: The Education of Children with Problems* by Nicholas J. Long and others
    b) *Reality Therapy* by William Glasser
    c) *Therapeutic Nursery School,* edited by Robert A. Furman, M.D., and Anny Katan, M.D.

2. See what motion pictures are available in your community. An excellent commercial film is *David and Lisa,* which would be particularly helpful for teachers on the secondary level. Your principal might arrange a showing for your school's entire staff.

3. Visit an accredited school for emotionally disturbed children. Observe there for a day and talk with different staff members.

As you follow up these activities, you will become increasingly aware that the behavior which angers you is a *signal* of an illness, just as red spots are a signal of measles. You will understand that a disturbed child does not have a disease of destroying property or hurting people; these are but symptoms of emotional disorder. And you will be reassured, once again, that *you are not responsible for the child's illness.*

The completion of step one (ascertaining that you'll be part of the solution, not the cause of the problem) and step two (becoming aware that emotional illness has deep environmental roots, that it is very complex, and that you alone won't "cure" it) frees you to ask the constructive "How can I help DC and thus help all of us in the group?" instead of the defensive "Why is she/he doing this to me?"

For a third positive step, read about the following classroom situations, imagining yourself as the teacher in each of the three.

Situation number one: As you sit with a reading circle, you see the children stop reading and begin to stare across the room at DC, who is drawing pictures on the floor with chalk.

Your response to help DC goes something like this. You say clearly, for all to hear, "DC, I'm unhappy because my reading students are looking at your pictures instead of at their books. Sarah (a dependable "normal"), will you help DC erase the chalk from the floor? Then you both may carry some books to the library for me."

Discipline in the Classroom

Comments:
1. DC is relieved because (a) DC's unacceptable behavior was clearly defined, and (b) provisions were made enabling DC to stop the behavior.
2. Sarah experiences an ego boost. She has helped another human, and thus her concept of self-worth is enhanced.
3. Other class members feel secure: DC's behavior did not take their teacher from them.
4. You enhance *your* self-concept by dealing constructively with a challenging situation.

Question: But DC had unmet needs! Shouldn't the child have been allowed to work them out on the floor with the chalk? The pictures weren't hurting anything!

Answer: Nonsense. DC's behavior was destroying the learning climate in your classroom. Furthermore, if DC had been permitted to continue unchecked, DC would have experienced progressive feelings of —

Guilt ("Teacher is mad at me. I'm bad.")
Panic ("Help! I'm losing control!")
ANGER ("Why won't someone *stop* me?")

Situation number two: DC keeps interrupting a small discussion group. You feel the children's annoyance at DC, and this intensifies your own impatience with DC's behavior.

You let the tone of your voice, as well as your words, communicate the group indignation. "DC, you're butting in and taking other people's turns. I don't like to have you take over while I'm talking! Now, I want you to get the card box so we can help you take turns. Okay?"

You know from experience that your students all enjoy this game. The card box referred to holds about 50 blank 3 x 2 cards. Each person receives the same agreed-upon number of cards, and every time a student speaks, she/he must put one of the cards back in the box. When someone's cards are used up, she/he cannot talk until everyone else's cards are gone. The students learn through trial and error how many times they are willing to permit DC to speak, and thus commit *themselves* to speaking.

Comments:
1. DC is grateful that unacceptable behavior was identified with honest directness. A disturbed child cannot tolerate a honey-sweet, "Let's not do that anymore," ladled out through clenched teeth. It comes through as, "I'm pretending to like you, but only because I'm afraid of my real thoughts. I wish you'd drop dead." The other students are also grateful because your acknowledgment of resentment

The Disturbed Child

allows them to feel comfortable with, instead of guilty about, their own anger toward DC.

2. Again you've given prompt assistance with impulse control, involving other group members. By playing a game that structures "equal rights," the pupils have a pleasurable as well as constructive role in helping their classmate.

3. You feel better and better. As you involve everyone in helping DC, it becomes "our" class instead of "my" class. A family bond begins to evolve.

Question: But DC is getting extra attention. Is that fair?

Answer: Who said life is fair? An emotionally ill person is a dependent person and requires extra attention. Don't you, as an adult, pay extra taxes to provide for patients in prisons and mental hospitals?

Situation number three: DC refuses to do a written assignment for the classroom.

Withdrawal behavior presents a special challenge. Your first response might well be to hypothesize *why* DC is refusing:

Too short an attention span? Call on a dependable pupil: "John, here is my stopwatch. Would you see how long it takes DC to complete the worksheet for today? DC, see if you can finish it before 10 minutes are up."

DC just can't do the work? "DC, I want you to do at least the first sentence now. I'll sit here and help you with it."

DC simply won't do the work? "DC, I'm sorry you aren't ready to write today. Maybe tomorrow you'll be able to." Coaxing or pleading will only reinforce the behavior you wish would go away.

Comment: Of course, there's a chance that none of these approaches will work. If the child shows total resistance, keep your cool and retreat for awhile.

Question: But doesn't that mean DC wins?

Answer: Wins? Who declared war? This child is *not* attacking you but, rather is engaged in self-protection from real or imagined danger.

Question: Well, after I've retreated for awhile, should I try again to get DC involved?

Answer: Of course. Does a doctor make out a single prescription and then abandon the patient if the medicine doesn't work?

In the above three incidents, you responded differently to different problems, but your approach each time included:

1. Stating clearly to the child what the child's inappropriate behavior consisted of
2. Identifying your own feelings about this behavior

Discipline in the Classroom

    3. Providing a supportive structure for a change of behavior

    4. Using, whenever appropriate, the participation of other students in this supportive structure.

Incorporating these basic steps, you can deal with a variety of disruptive classroom situations. DC can be a girl as easily as a boy, of course. While statistically we have more disturbed boys than girls, how many giggly girls disrupt a lesson because they were brought up as "first a female," while they heard their brothers challenged to be "serious students?"

Or instead of being age 10, DC could be 4 or 14. Although DC may be emotionally ill, a high school student has to have mastered a fair amount of impulse control to survive in that structure. Also, DC's behavior could take the form of *repression* of hostile feelings rather than expression of them. A silent resister can sometimes hold up group effort more effectively than the loud-mouthed extrovert.

One unholy situation which has not been discussed is what to do when a number of DC's are placed in your already overcrowded classroom. In my opinion, you'll have to give up. The only question is how you go about throwing in the sponge.

In the foregoing discussion, our disturbed child was compartmentalized as though different from his peers. In reality, no clear line can be drawn between "healthy" behavior and that which isn't so healthy. All students move up and down their own individual continuum of neurotic responses which they employ to master a particular environment at a particular time. But the disturbed child makes *compulsive responses* which occur *day after day* and which *interfere regularly* with classroom goals.

As long as teachers are asked to control sick psyches while teaching subject matter, they will have cause for deep frustration. There are no easy solutions.

Discipline and Human Needs

Discipline Is Caring

Alvin W. Howard

Ask any teacher, beginning or experienced, what the biggest difficulty with children is and she or he will almost certainly answer, "Discipline and classroom control." As the second major difficulty, the teacher will probably cite student achievement or lack of it in school, a problem closely related to discipline.

Good discipline is important because no group of people can work together successfully without establishing standards of behavior, mutual respect, and a desirable system of values that leads each person in the group to develop self-control and self-direction.

Good discipline does *not* result if a teacher adopts an inflexible punitive approach or if a teacher is too permissive, pretending that annoying behavior does not exist. In *Schools Without Failure*, William Glasser points out that those who would completely eliminate or substantially relax rules in their eagerness to please children don't realize that firm and fair policies of discipline indicate that adults care about young people and that children may interpret the reverse as a symptom of lack of interest in them.

In their relations with pupils, teachers should be firm, fair, and friendly. Teachers need to take firm positions on many things, but before they do they must determine what they individually stand for or against and what that stand implies. Firmness does not imply rigid domination of children nor does it require snarling and growling at them to cow them into submission. Authoritarianism breeds resentment; taking a "Do this or else" position can be exactly the wrong thing for a teacher to do. (For example, a beginning teacher told Dick, a large eighth grader, to take his seat or go to the office. He did neither, and the teacher could not physically compel Dick to obey her. So, she sent for the principal who, after a quick appraisal of the situation, said, "Come, Dick, you and I need to talk about this someplace else.")

Most children have a keen sense of fair play. A pupil who does something wrong expects to bear the consequences but also expects anyone else who commits the same offense to receive the same treat-

Discipline in the Classroom

ment. A teacher should not play favorites or punish the entire class for the sins of a few (e.g., mass detention). A better method is to have a private conference with the erring child as soon as possible about the problem. At best, detention, whether for one student or for many, is of dubious value.

Teachers should be scrupulously fair and courteous—especially if they expect similar treatment. Teachers who make wisecracks or are flip or arrogant can expect the same from their students and are not justified in resenting their students' attitude. (Each day, Mr. Johnson, a first year teacher, sent a large number of students to the office for "smarting off." Yet, when the counselor pointed out to him that virtually every youngster complained that Mr. Johnson talked that way to them, the teacher was indignant.)

A teacher should demonstrate friendliness by being understanding, tolerant, and sincere with students. Efforts by a teacher to be one of the gang are seldom, if ever, successful and often prevent development of an atmosphere of mutual respect that is conducive to learning. The teacher who adopts the slang, customs, and behavior of students will discover that they may be amused or offended by the teacher's actions or contemptuous of them. (A group of girls in one home economics class requested a different teacher because theirs was so "cutesy.")

Some discipline problems, hopefully minor ones, come up in every classroom. But minor problems aren't likely to become major ones if a teacher remembers the following guidelines:

1. Work at being the kind of person children like and trust, and remember that everyone needs success—particularly those with a record of failure. Maintain the respect of the class without being condescending. (Gary, a large sixth grader who had been sent to the office for his "noncooperative" attitude, told the principal he wouldn't respond to his teacher's questions as long as he had to tell his answers to her clown hand puppet.)

2. Maintain a cheerful and attractive classroom rather than a disorderly one which might encourage unruly behavior. Also, remember that a pleasant voice, a neat appearance, and a positive attitude are contagious.

3. Get to know your students. Teachers who know their students soon develop almost a sixth sense for anticipating trouble before it begins. Good teachers report that students frequently believe them to have eyes in the back of their heads.

4. Be enthusiastic and courteous and keep your sense of humor. Teachers who really believe that children and learning are important tend to be enthusiastic, and that enthusiasm is contagious. Be as

courteous to your class as you wish them to be with you. Also, don't "see" everything that happens; learn to ignore some things and laugh at others.

5. Make education interesting and relevant to children's lives. Teachers who believe they can get by without planning may get away with it temporarily, but before long lack of organization and imagination will produce dreary lessons, student restiveness, increasing discontent, and ultimate chaos. My guess is that the largest number of classroom offenses occur because the curriculum is dull and the teacher has planned poorly.

6. Don't use schoolwork as punishment. (Linda told her mother that she hated both school and her fifth grade teacher. "Every time we forget to act like prisoners in a reform school," she said, "we have more written work.") Give reasonable assignments, and don't be vague and ambiguous when giving directions.

7. Never use threats in an effort to enforce discipline. What will you do if a child takes up the challenge—as someone ultimately will? A threat that is not carried out only makes the teacher look foolish. (For example, a teacher threatening to read aloud confiscated notes may end up in confrontation with a militant who refuses to part with a note, or a teacher looking silly after reading aloud a note that proves to be a deliberate plant.)

8. Never humiliate a child. Publicly scolding or ridiculing students will make them bitter and will probably turn the rest of the class against the teacher. (A ninth-grade teacher sharpened the fine-honed edge of his tongue against a borderline dropout. When the boy did drop out of school, the class was extremely antagonistic to the teacher for the remainder of the year.)

9. Don't strong arm students. (A high school physical education instructor abruptly seized a tenth-grade boy by the left arm, demanding, "Where do you think you're going?" The boy spun with the pull and landed a looping right hook between the teacher's eyes, breaking his nose and knocking him out.)

10. Avoid arguing with your pupils. Discussions about classwork are invaluable, but arguments that become emotional encounters with pupil freedom fighters create ill will on both sides, sometimes with rather surprising side effects. (The group of seventh graders who requested that they be transferred to another class because all they ever did was argue with their teacher knew the difference between discussion and argument.)

11. Don't act as though you expect trouble or you will almost certainly encounter some. (Mr. Potter consistently reported Bennie as a troublemaker, although no other teacher did. Bennie reported, "No matter what I do for Mr. Potter, it's wrong." Mr. Potter ex-

plained, "I had Bennie's brother two years ago, and he was a troublemaker. I told Bennie the first day of school that I wouldn't put up with any nonsense from him.")

12. Let students know you care. Caring means determining, preferably jointly with the class, what is acceptable and what is not, both in terms of behavior and achievement, continually keeping in mind that all children differ and that what is reasonable and acceptable with one group may not be with another.

Caring means that you are interested in what your students have to say even though it may not pertain directly to the lesson and that you must forego doing all the talking.

13. Establish as few rules as possible and keep them as simple as possible. Examine them carefully from time to time and eliminate those that are unnecessary. (For years, one school enforced a rule that no club could meet on Thursday afternoons. When a new teacher asked why this was so, no one could give a reason. Eventually someone remembered that a long-extinct service organization had conducted activities for children in a nearby building on Thursday afternoons.)

14. Expect to handle the normal kinds of misbehavior yourself, but seek assistance for those problems that need the skills of a specialist.

My First Year of Teaching

Wylie Crawford

After a full week of teacher orientation workshops, I made my teaching debut. I had just finished a year of study at the University of Chicago and was ready to try out some of the theories and dime store philosophies that I had come across during the past year, one of which was that teaching was simply the other side of the coin from studying.

One of the first sources of confusion in my new job dealt with organizational structure. The school where I taught was a lower-middle class suburban public school which employed various innovative techniques in order to achieve the personal development of both the students and the teachers. In order to do this, it allowed considerable flexibility in the use of facilities, course scheduling, and study requirements. The school stressed the development of the individual, but it also used team teaching.

Aside from these structural-organizational concerns, I was apprehensive about the whole subject of control of large quantities of potentially hostile students. My past experience offered no illumination on this account.

How was I going to talk to them? Could I be relaxed and a "pal"? Or an authoritarian and hard-nosed dictator? I doubted if I could pull off the latter, and certainly the former seemed more in keeping with the school's philosophy.

I had resolved ahead of time that the best method at first would be to establish myself as a "significant other," that is, someone to be reckoned with. Past experience as a student had shown me that teachers who were not "significant others" were not effective in maintaining either student attention or interest. They were teachers who had been judged unworthy of respect either through their weakness, their injustice, or their ignorance of subject matter.

Excerpted with permission from "The Other Side of the Coin," an article in *Don't Smile Until Christmas: Accounts of the First Year of Teaching*, edited by Kevin Ryan. © 1970 by the University of Chicago Press. All rights reserved. Reprinted by permission.

Discipline in the Classroom

I approached the first days of class with many preconceptions floating around in my mind and with a mixed bag of emotions (and indescribable gastric distress attributable to the long drive to school, the early homeroom, and the first days). Chaos threatened during the first week or so. The physics course was not too much trouble, since physics was my major field in college. Most of my initial activities in physics involved making up a course outline for each topic. The general science was another story, however. Hours were spent in trying either to comprehend or to create materials for this course.

Throughout the year, it was a continual race to keep ahead of the students in these varied and unfamiliar topics. As a result, it was not until well into October that I found enough time or energy to devote to the more personal and rewarding activities of the teacher: talking to students and other teachers during free time, sitting back and looking at where I was going, and making connections between 300 names and 300 people in front of me.

The latter was no mean task. The traditional name-learning aids used in other schools unfortunately were not available in a team-teaching situation. A seating chart (for the large-group instruction) was made up, but was too big to be useful, and there were no fixed seats in the other activities (labs, seminars, independent study). Students met during the week in varying combinations and at irregular intervals, so that some students were very familiar and others were nearly anonymous. After a while, of course, most of the names became associated with faces, but this process took longer than it would have in a traditional school. The names, I might add, were learned in the nick of time. I had the majority of them down pat just as I realized that my control problems were beginning to show.

In the beginning, my fears about discipline and class control were abated. Instead of finding students who were organized for an all-out, massed offensive, I found students who wished for the most part to be left alone; instead of finding students who were outspoken and arrogant, I found students who were yielding and eager not to "make waves." For the first week or two, the vast majority of my students just sat, seemed to listen attentively, and asked questions when called for. All was sweetness and light, it seemed—except that, at times, I felt like a leper. As I walked through the halls or independent study areas, I was aware that I was being sized up. I was being regarded with side-long glances—both curious and fearful—which seemed to ask: "Is he a murderer or just a strapper?"

This was somewhat disarming, since my idea of becoming a "significant other" was to have the class feel at home with me and like me, so that if the going ever got rough during the year, I would be able to recall the pleasant days, when we were all friends, and

First Year

emotionally blackmail them into wanting things that way again. But this approach couldn't work, of course, if they were convinced from the start that I was another ogre just like those of their grade school days. I was determined to win them over by personality, however, contrary to the advice from one of the more experienced (and cynical) teachers who warned: "Don't smile until Christmas."

My colleague's advice was not taken, of course, since my ideal classroom was one in which everyone was happy, where everyone felt free to speak out when he had something important to say, without fear from harsh criticism or ridicule from me or from his fellows. To create such a situation, it was only natural to smile, and so I did. And eventually, the class did too, but in a slightly different way.

As the first month passed, the routine and boredom of even this school began to set in. The happy, relaxed, loosely disciplined class which I saw developing began to take strange and subtle turns in the wrong directions. The students were not just happy and relaxed, they were content and almost asleep.

I started to get the message: their natural curiosity had not been aroused. I tried to spice up my presentations and asked more questions of individuals in the class, but this seemed to no avail. The symptoms persisted—one student would be looking out the window; another student would be sitting on a table when there were chairs still available; two girls would be gossiping just a little too loud, and would continue even when I stood right next to them.

While these were noticeable changes, no one of them was objectionable enough to make a big fuss about. After all, my own concept of the ideal classroom atmosphere was broad enough to allow for occasional uninterested students. There would be days when they, too, would become involved and some other students would lose interest. Treating the students as adults, I felt that they knew they were pushing my patience a bit and that a gentle reminder would be sufficient to set things straight. And it did, for a while. But soon I found myself giving mild admonishments more and more often, and always to the same small group of offenders.

Now, instead of just looking out the window, they were waving to passing cars. Instead of just sitting on the tables, a few were sprawled out on them. My resolve was still not shaken. After all, I had expected much worse, and we were still getting used to each other. When they saw the folly of it all, our little testing period would be over.

In reality, as far as the students were concerned, the testing period was already over, and they had won the game. I was going to be a pushover. And, since the other students had been watching the events of the first month, my list of offenders got longer as my blood

Discipline in the Classroom

pressure got higher. The situation got to the point where I had to brace myself before walking into certain particularly "liberated" classes. But one day when I was not mentally braced for the usual harassments, I did what came naturally and gave them a thorough chewing-out. I'm sure it was too emotional, but it worked. A month before, I would have considered it an unnecessary act, and a sign of failure. But now, it seemed the only thing to do. I had been poisoned and insulted by their giggles and inattentions long enough.

After this incident, I felt that things would simmer down, which they did for a while. But when trouble began to brew again, I asked each individual in the little core group of five to meet me after school for a five-minute conference. All agreed to come, but only one showed up. I was obviously still not a "significant other" for them.

The delinquent four received one-hour detentions, the first detentions I had given that year. I was not proud to have given them, but my patience and resources had run out. I was glad that this procedure was available to me, since I had dug myself such a deep hole that I needed some show of external authority to help me begin the return to sanity.

This was only a beginning. There were endless tests to my authority throughout the year. Somehow, my chosen initial approach to classroom control seemed to extend my testing period indefinitely. Throughout the year I felt that I had to prove over and over again that I really was a teacher, and not just the good-natured boob I had seemed at the beginning of the year.

It seemed that since I at first chose not to use the facial expressions, verbal barbs, and peer pressures that every "real" teacher uses, I could never use them effectively in the students' eyes. I concluded that for me to eventually "break the rules" and do what I really wanted to do with the class, I first had to learn those rules very well.

Embarrassment and Ridicule

Lawrence E. Vredevoe

SOME TEACHERS and administrators seem to feel that a pupil will correct his ways if he is embarrassed or ridiculed before his classmates. I am certain, however, that although remarks like, "Don't keep acting like a kindergartner" or "How would you like to go down to your little sister's room?" may temporarily stop the undesirable action of a pupil, they more frequently cause new problems and do more harm than good.

Some pupils laugh at the ridicule, which disturbs the whole class, but other pupils rally to the support of their shamed classmates, feeling that the teacher has taken unfair advantage of him.

The victim himself, even though he may appear to be the tough type who can laugh the whole thing off, feels bitter toward the teacher. Some pupils who were interviewed after having been subjected to ridicule made comments like the following:

"I could have killed her."

"The teacher can say anything and make you feel cheap, but you can never answer back."

"I lost all interest in this joint after being made fun of in his class."

The teacher who employs ridicule and embarrassment alienates the whole class and humiliates individual members. Furthermore, on occasion these weapons have a boomerang action.

To the question, "Do you want me to send you to the first-grade room?" one student replied, "Anything to get out of here."

An elderly teacher who took seventh graders on her lap to embarrass them was herself acutely embarrassed when one pupil put his arms around her neck and kissed her.

Another teacher made a pupil get under her desk because he was such a disgrace to the group. Later she forgot he was under there and sat at her desk not realizing why her third graders were convulsed.

Discipline in the Classroom

All teachers on all levels would do well to count the costs before resorting to embarrassment or ridicule in the classroom or before any group.

Teachers with the best classroom control report that they seldom if ever resort to these methods. One such teacher who was challenged by a colleague for disdaining to use sarcasm or ridicule replied, "I am an adult and I can take it, but I am not sure what harm I may do a child by embarrassing him, so I use other methods."

Classroom control is frequently difficult, and some disciplinary methods must be employed. However, embarrassment and ridicule are not only coward's tools, they are weapons which may wound deeply or be turned against the teacher.

Wanted

Henrietta M. Krahulik

The boy seemed to be a permanent resident of the small room set aside for chronic discipline cases. He'd dressed his grasshopper frame in clothes that begged for attention: clompy boots, jeans as tight as curtains on curtain stretchers, and a streaked Che Guevara-type jacket. The once blue jacket and jeans may have had a run-in with bleach and come off second best. That hair! Surely that black thatch caused him to see through his glasses darkly.

Once as I passed, February's thin sunlight and the office window's grillwork conspired to throw bars across the glassed-in boy. Why, he's in a cage — probably a cage of his own making, I amended.

"Who's the boy in solitary?" I asked Mr. Patman, boys' counselor.

"You're new, Mrs. Krahulik, or you'd know he's Joe O'Mara, the reason teachers climb walls or become teaching dropouts. Sad case."

"Yes?" I encouraged.

"One word describes Joe: unwanted. He was an unwanted baby; his mother told us so. He's been unwanted in classes, from kindergarten on. Not forever, though, will Joe be unwanted. He's headed for top billing on the 'Most Wanted' posters that decorate post offices. He's fourteen now. When he was five, his baby sister was killed in a fire in the home. His parents think Joe was playing with matches before the fire started."

"Guilt-edged?"

"Maybe. Joe's parents — solid, middle-income people — have had him probed and dissected by child psychologists. Their comments: 'hostile, masochistic, begs to be caught....'"

"According to Skinnerian psychology," I said, "whatever gives pleasurable reinforcement tends to result in repetition of an activity. We're *pleading for encores* from our compulsive show-off!"

With the zeal of a conservationist, I exhort. "Save the unwanted!" So the next day I told Mr. Patman, "I want him."

"Whoa, back up. Who, what, when?"

"Joe, English 7, tomorrow."

"You feel OK?"

Discipline in the Classroom

Joe echoed Bill Patman's concern for my health. "You crazy?"

"I hope not. I said I have a homestead staked out for you in B105."

"Why?" Joe stood stiff-legged and bristling, a hound dog sizing up a porcupine.

"Why ask why?" I countered. "Come, settle." Settle he did, flaunting his badge of garish clothes. For two weeks he held his cockiness in tight rein. Then one day he muttered, "Dullsville," and fell asleep.

"Nudge him, Bart. Joe, you forgot to tell us 'good night.'" What a charming grin!

Assuming that every adolescent is a Ptolemy, the center of his own universe, I reasoned: A boy who gets his kicks from losing might satisfy his need for ridicule by means of an appropriate surrogate. So... I gave Joe the task of writing a first-person-singular narrative in which the first-person-singular was a ridiculous lout. Joe created a character who was the fall guy, and Joe, as author, was freed to work constructively. Successful.

If I could graph Joe's progress like a chart, I would label February a success peak. March would be a chasm. "Joe's suspended," Kim reported. "Someone mouthed off about his horrible jacket."

Had Joe reverted to his old behavior pattern, become a—what is the word—recidivist? He had. When he returned to class, his go-slow approach to grand-standing shifted to full speed ahead. The class exercised Spartan-like restraint, and I followed William James' advice: "The art of being wise is the art of knowing what to overlook."

April began as a rerun of March. Another suspension. "Joe goes in and out of school like he's caught in a revolving door," Jake remarked.

Expecting to reclaim Joe this time was as unrealistic as expecting to smuggle morning past a rooster. I tried, but the students, at best lukewarm to Joe, now openly resented him. "We enjoy this class," several said, "when Joe's gone." Joe overheard.

When the humidity thickens, clouds darken, and lightning flickers, Hoosiers begin an anxious sky watch. Tornadoes are aborning.

The big blow struck April 21. I entered fifth period and found a free-for-all in full swing. Root of touble? Joe (who else?) and his philosophy: "Do unto other before they can do unto you." Somehow I steered the class into discussing various plans for April 22, Earth Day.

I seemed calm, but I waged silent war. With various devices, I countered Joe's periodic bids for attention: slammed-down books, raspy throat clearings, humming. First came the evil glare I'd perfected in front of my bathroom mirror. (My eye control is a talent I'm proud of; it saves voice and feet.) Joe grinned back. Next came my very nasty glare, which I reinforced by jabbing my finger unmistakably at Joe. He yawned.

The class ignored him. They suggested several projects for April 22: boycott buses and walk to school, demolish and bury an old junker.

"Earth Day, not Mirth Day," I cautioned. They agreed on a sensible litter-cleanup project and arranged to work in special groups, pointedly excluding Joe. Joe's thrust was stilletto-sharp. "How old are you? Sixty?"

"Not quite."

"You gonna send me to the office?"

"No. I took you for better or worse until June do us part."

"I'll keep causing trouble. What're you gonna do about it?"

"Something drastic."

"Like hitting me?" He whipped off his glasses. "C'mon, hit me!"

What a porcupine-baitin' hound dog! To gain composure, I applied fresh lipstick, vivid red, a shade unfashionable this year. I advanced toward Joe, smilingly pleasant. Pleasant? I was brewing the blackest thoughts.

"You crazy?" Joe muttered.

Yes, crazy to bother with you, you insolent, incorrigible pipsqueak. Marianne giggled nervously. Feet shuffled; the clock wheezed. Cafeteria whiffs drifted in—spaghetti? There was a somnambulistic unreality about it all. I wanted to slap that smirking face, to slap and slap and slap.

Joe had leaned back in his seat. I bent over his upturned face, our eyes locked, and I saw myself reflected in the eyes of a wayward, troubled boy.

He made everything that was made and found it good, very good. Good, in the beginning, but along the way....

Joe tensed for my blow.

Along the way we despoil—the good earth, one another, ourselves.

I brushed Joe's hair back and branded his forehead with my fiery lipstick. I kissed Joe.

The class exploded in a bombshell of laughter that was a close cousin to hysteria. Down Joe's cheeks trickled two fat tears, a torrent, and he slumped onto his desk, sobbing.

As abruptly as if a machine had been switched off, the laughter stopped. I shoved a rest-room pass to Joe. He fled.

"Hey, he's not so tough," Jackie marveled.

Discipline in the Classroom

"Joe's like a thin-shelled egg," I said, "seemingly impervious but inwardly fragile."

"Let's include him in our Earth Day cleanup."

The next day a sneaker-shod, jacket-shed Joe sidled into the room. "Am I welcome, Ma'am?" (I'm sorry, his tone said.)

"Welcome, Son."

April 22, Earth Day, Joe's rebirthday? It's up to Joe. He was weighed by his peers and, on that day, was found wanted.

Acknowledgments

Discipline: An Overview

"Discipline Is . . . ." by Sister Helena Brand, SNJM, college professor of English.
"What the Books Don't Tell You" by Jane Tylor Field, high school teacher and writer.
"A Positive Approach to Elementary School Discipline" by Frances Holliday, university professor emeritus of education.
"Classroom Control in the High School" by Emelie Ruth Dodge, high school teacher of English.
"Secondary School Discipline" by Knute Larson, writer; Frances D. Bartlett and Matilda Luney, high school teachers.

Curriculum as Discipline

"Better Curriculum—Better Discipline" by William Van Til, university professor of education.
"Operating a Free but Disciplined Classroom" by Daisy Bortz, elementary school teacher, as told to Anne Hoppock, state administrator.
"Reading: Failure and Delinquency" by William C. Kvaraceus, university professor of education.

Classroom Techniques for Discipline

"Matching Teacher, Student, and Method" by Louis J. Rubin, university professor of education.
"Cheating" by John Carter Weldon, community college instructor in French.
"The Teacher and Preventive Discipline" by Adah Peckenpaugh, high school teacher of English.
"A Lesson in Discipline" by Teresa Foley, elementary school teacher.

Methods of Structuring Classroom Behavior

"Behavior Modification" by the Staff of the Center for Studies of Child and Family Mental Health, National Institute of Mental Health, Bethesda, Maryland.
"A Positive Approach to Disruptive Behavior" by Teressa Marjorie Pratt, educational consultant for specific learning disabilities.
"The Disturbed Child in the Classroom" by Katharine F. Tift, research and development in drug-related problems.

Discipline and Human Needs

"Discipline Is Caring" by Alvin W. Howard, university professor of education.
"My First Year of Teaching" by Wylie Crawford, computer systems engineer.
"Embarrassment and Ridicule" by Lawrence E. Vredevoe, university professor of education.
"Wanted" by Henrietta M. Krahulik, junior high school teacher.

All articles in this book have been reprinted with the permission of *Today's Education*.

DEC 20 1974
DISCHARGED

DISCHARGED 1975
OCT 30

DISCHARGED
DISCHARGED

NOV 15 1975
DISCHARGED
DISCHARGED
DISCHARGED

MAR 10 1976
DISCHARGED
MAR 24 1976

APR 15 1976
DISCHARGED

DISCHARGED 1977

MAR 21 1977
MAR 28 1977
APR 5 1977
DISCHARGED

FEB 10 1978

APR 22 1978

DISCHARGED 1988

DISCHARGED

DISCHARGED 1977

NOV 20 1978
DISCHARGED

MAR 29 1979

DISCHARGED 1979
APR 23 1979

DISCHARGED

DISCHARGED

APR 22 1980
DISCHARGED

NOV 12 1981
DISCHARGED

DISCHARGED

DISCHARGED 1984

MAR 10 1987

OCT 22 1990

DISCHARGED 1991

APR 23 1980
DISCHARGED 1980
NOV 19 1981
DISCHARGED
APR 12 1982
APR 20 1982
MAY 15 1982
DISCHARGED

JUL 11 1987
APR 1983
MAY 5 1983
JUL 13 1983
DISCHARGED
APR 11 1984
JUL 9 1985

NOV 5 1989